# ON RESISTANCE: A MANIFESTO

**ALSO BY CURTIS WHITE**

Heretical Songs

Metaphysics in the Midwest

The Idea of Home

Anarcho-Hindu

Memories of My Father Watching TV

Requiem

America's Magic Mountain

The Middle Mind

The Spirit of Disobedience

The Barbaric Heart

The Science Delusion

We, Robots

Lacking Character

Living in a World that Can't Be Fixed

Transcendent

# ON RESISTANCE

## A MANIFESTO

CURTIS WHITE

MELVILLE HOUSE
BROOKLYN • LONDON

**ON RESISTANCE : A MANIFESTO**

First published in 2026 by Melville House

First Melville House Printing: June 2026
Distributed by Penguin Random House LLC, 1745 Broadway, New York, NY 10019 USA. www.penguinrandomhouse.com

Melville House Publishing
46 John Street
Brooklyn, NY 11201
and
Melville House UK
Suite 2000
16/18 Woodford Road
London E7 0HA

mhpbooks.com
@melvillehouse

ISBN: 978-1-68589-269-2
ISBN: 978-1-68589-270-8 (eBook)

Library of Congress Control Number: 2025948130

Printed in the United States of America
1 3 5 7 9 10 8 6 4 2

A catalog record for this book is available from the Library of Congress

The authorized representative in the EU for product safety and compliance is Easy Access System Europe, Mustamäe tee 50, 10621 Tallinn, Estonia. gpsr.requests@easproject.com

In memoriam

Lewis Lapham
1935–2024

John Barth
1930–2024

## CONTENTS

# INTRODUCTION

## PSYCHIC TREASON

I am living in a world that no longer exists.

I once lived in a vital world whose only limit was no limit, "free frame of reference," as the Haight Street Diggers thought. It was a world of beatniks, Buddhists, hippies, free-jazz poets, pacifists, wandering guitar soloists, postmodern fabulists, soulful anarchists, and collaborative maunderers. It was also a world of close readers, deconstructionists, and afficionados of the beautiful, all performing in the heady atmosphere of refusal, a general strike of the Imagination.

It was the rebirth of the romantics, bohemians, Poets with a capital *P*, and Oscar Wildean dandies. In the face of the work ethic, bohemians old and new had the "right to be lazy," as Marx's son-in-law Paul Lafargue declared, or the right to "do your own thing," as freak culture would later agree. Of course, this is not a description of a real world, "how it was back then," but of a psychic climate, the lovely mists and roiling waters of which still sustain my inner life. As Ted Gioia writes in his book *Music: A Subversive History*, the era brought "a highly contagious psychic treason to prevailing values."

This world and its open assumptions about possibility slowly dissipated over a thirty-year period. As the late Sly Stone put it, "The possibility of possibility was leaking out." It seemed quite dead by the millennium, our collective mind aspirated into glass pipettes by techno-oligarchs who bore us no love. We were left with Data World, the Great American Smartphone Society. We have been priced out of cities, so there are no avenues to barricade, no "scenes" where artists and musicians can hang out, and our universities are in ruin, occupied by "indentured students," in Elizabeth Tandy Shermer's telling phrase, studying only what the boss wants. And what the boss wants has nothing to do with poets. Even at Christ Church University in Canterbury, the destination for Chaucer's pilgrims in *The Canterbury Tales*, poetry is "no longer viable in the current climate."

And yet my heart/mind still resides in that other world, that yesterday world, the world that no longer exists.

Whatever for?

Of course, the feeling of living in a non-existent world is not a new thing. Every human life that goes beyond the thirtieth year will be familiar with it to some degree. The Austrian writer Stefan Zweig wrote a book about it, *The World of Yesterday*.

For Zweig, that meant late-nineteenth- and early-twentieth-century Europe and its generation of elite artists and intellectuals like Freud, the novelist Romain Rolland, and the modernist composer Richard Strauss. But in 1939, after the rise of Hitler, Zweig and his wife, Lotte, went into exile not only from Austria but from a world rich with music, words, images, and ideas. His novels had been placed on the Nazi's list of proscribed books and burned, and it was increasingly clear that, as a Jew, he himself was likely on a different and deadlier list. They went to London first, then to the United States, where they were guests of Yale University, and finally to a small German colony in Petrópolis, Brazil, of all unlikely and far-flung places for a Viennese aesthete. In 1942, he committed suicide with his wife by an overdose of sleeping pills. As he explained in a note, "I think it better to conclude in good time and in erect bearing a life in which intellectual labor meant the purest joy."

A photograph was taken of the bodies of Zweig and Lotte lying on a small bed. He is shaved, mustache neatly trimmed, in a shirt and tie. She is in fetal posture, snuggled at his side, as if they were just napping after sex, or as if patiently waiting for whatever life came next. Her left hand covers and comforts his folded hands. The fatal box of sleeping pills sits on the bedside table beside a water glass. There is no book on the table for bedtime reading. No need for that any longer. Zweig had sent the manuscript of *The World of Yesterday* to his publisher the previous day. Everything is tidy, nothing left undone, except all the things he might have done had he chosen to live. Suicide was Zweig's way of checking out of the grand fantasy of cosmopolitan Europe, soon to become a mass grave.

Also in 1939, the first year of Zweig's exile, Jean Renoir's movie *The Rules of the Game* was released. It tells the story of that historical moment, Germany and France once again on the threshold of war, but in a different way. Rather than mourning the death of Europe's rich culture, Renoir suggests that Zweig's privileged class was to a degree responsible for the nearing catastrophe.

The film takes place at a country estate called La Colinière among members of the *haute bourgeoisie.* This is the stage for Renoir's display of the upper-crust's moral indifference to everyone and everything (especially rabbits) outside of their own class. For them, life is simply the "rules of the game" that apply inside of their caste. As the character Octave explains, "You see, in this world, there is one awful thing, and that is that everyone has his reasons." In other words, everyone knows the rules/reasons of the social class game, even if it is inhuman to follow them. As Renoir explained:

> What is interesting about this film, perhaps, is the moment when it was made. It was shot between Munich and the war, and I shot it absolutely impressed, absolutely disturbed by the state of mind of a part of French society, a part of English society, a part of world society.

*The Rules of the Game* is not a tragedy but a terminal comedy. It is a farewell party. It is "laughter out of dead bellies," in Ezra Pound's phrase.

Zweig was of the "state of mind" that Renoir describes. Zweig confesses that the intellectual elite of Vienna were not awake to the rough beast slouching toward them. Zweig writes, "We noticed little of these dangerous changes in our native land; our eyes were bent entirely on books and pictures." In Nietzsche's words, Zweig lived "in a happy blindness between the past and the future."

*The World of Yesterday* is an acknowledgment that this abundance of culture, all these erudite manners, the strict enforcement of elite conduct, all this endless elaboration and haughty indifference, would soon be, literally, ash in the wind. Like so many at the time, Zweig was in exile not only from his home, but from everything he had taken to be reality, and he was incapable of imagining a new reality. For Zweig, suicide was nothing because his world was already dead. He was a victim of history twice over: as a refugee and as someone who could not live beyond the memory of a world that no longer existed. As Nietzsche wrote in *The Use and Abuse of History*, an obsession with the past destroys the possibility of a living present:

> One who cannot . . . forget the past, who cannot stand on a single point, like a goddess of victory, without fear or giddiness, will never know what happiness is; and, worse still, will never do anything to make others happy.

On the other hand, Renoir was one who could see the history that Zweig was ruined by but then proceed to the next "joyful deed," the making of a work of art. Renoir was Zweig's health-giving opposite, a rule-breaker and a world-maker. As the British *Socialist Worker* described his work in 2006:

> [The] great quality in Renoir's movies is that he is always a rebel. In Renoir's movie world, rules are for breaking, conventions are for disregarding, and authority is for mocking.

In our own very much more dangerous world—threatened not only by fascism but also by nuclear annihilation, climate disruption, spreading food deserts, and ever-larger and more desperate masses of migrants—we too fail to see the writing on the wall even though, once again, it is right before us in "letters of fire," as Zweig wrote. Worse, it is not at all clear that we can do what Nietzsche thought was crucial: "to assimilate and digest the past and turn it to sap."

Happily, it will always be possible to create stories that liberate us from the stories of our masters. This is what William Blake called for when he wrote in *Jerusalem* (1804),

"I *must* create a system or be *enslaved* by another *man's*; I will not reason and compare: my business is to create." Or, even more assertively, William Carlos Williams in *Kora in Hell* (1920):

> There is nothing sacred about literature, it is damned from one end to the other. There is nothing in literature but change and change is mockery. I'll write whatever I damn please, whenever I damn please and as I damn please and it'll be good if the authentic spirit of change is on it.

That, for me, has always been gospel.

Blake's quote is "heavy," as hippies used to say, because it asks, as Tolstoy put it, "What is to be done?" The answer to that question might simply be "tell better stories." Live through better stories. Live through stories that will be understood in an as yet unimagined world, just past the next bend in the river, where the Imagination lives in all its inherited riches. So, let us be Nietzschean, all too Nietzschean, without fear or giddiness, and seek liberation for ourselves and others.

# ON RESISTANCE

# TELL BETTER STORIES

Whoever can give his people better stories than the ones they live in is like the priest in whose hands common bread and wine become capable of feeding the very soul.

—Hugh Kenner, *The Pound Era*

# THE PHILANTHROPIC INDUSTRIAL COMPLEX

Before we can begin to tell our own stories, we must first un-tell the stories that hold us "everywhere in chains," in Jean-Jacques Rousseau's ever-revealing phrase. The first of those stories to be un-told, the first line of the status quo's ideological defense, is this: "You have no need for 'resistance' because we have already provided it for you. Yes, there are problems, the poor are ever with us, but we are philanthropic, we are lovers of humanity, and we will create charitable foundations to prove it."

In the fall of 2009, I was approached by Hal Clifford, editor at *Orion* magazine, and asked to write an essay about American philanthropy, especially in relation to environmentalism. From the first I had doubts about the assignment. I said, "Not-for-profit organizations like yours cannot afford to attack philanthropy because if you attack one foundation you may as well attack them all. You'll be cutting your own throat."

Hal assured me that while all this might be true someone had to take up the issue, and *Orion* was willing to do so. And I was the right person to write the essay precisely because I was not an insider but simply an honest intelligence. So, with many misgivings, I said I'd try.

I interviewed about a dozen people on both sides of the field, both givers and getters. The people I spoke to were eager to articulate their grievances even if they were just as eager to be anonymous. I also should acknowledge that the development of these grievances was no doubt colored by my own experiences as a board member and president of the board of two not-for-profit literary organizations.

I had worked for several months writing and revising the essay when Hal Clifford announced that he would be leaving *Orion*. My first thought was "uh-oh." The managing editor, Chip Blake, took over my essay and at that point things got dicey. Ultimately, he explained that he hadn't been fully aware of my assignment, that he hadn't known the essay would be an attack on "the oligarchy," that it didn't seem to be fully a part of the magazine's usual interests, and that—fatally—from the magazine's point of view publishing the essay would be an exercise in "self-mutilation." Exactly what I had said at the beginning! They had come to their senses, even if it had taken a long time and cost me a lot of work to get there.

Secretly, though, I was pleased. This editorial catastrophe was the best possible confirmation of everything I argue in the essay.

In the United States, everyone may enjoy freedom of speech so long as it doesn't matter. For those who would like what they say to matter, freedom of speech is very expensive. It is for this reason that organizations with a strong sense of public mission but not much money are dependent on the blonde child of capitalism, private philanthropy. Working with this child has its challenges, not the least of which is the risk that the philanthropist will end up dominating the mission of the organizations it funds. According to one source with decades of experience in philanthropy, foundation grants are too often a drama between "gods" and the "little people" who fulfill the destiny of the gods.

Like the system of patronage that served the arts and charity from the Renaissance through the eighteenth century, private foundations have the rarest privilege of all: They do not have to explain themselves. They do not have to justify the origins of their wealth, or how they use that wealth, or what the real benefit of their largesse is. To quote an unlikely source, Steve Forbes has written that "there is one, largely unaccountable aristocracy in American life today: foundations . . . They do not answer to the marketplace or an electorate."

Generally speaking, private philanthropy gets a pass in the press. I assume that journalists think they have better things to do than criticize rich people for giving their money away, especially when they are funding good causes. But even if it has been mostly voiced off the public stage, criticism of the culture of philanthropy in America, from both the left and the right, cuts deep. Foundations have been described by both wings of American politics as arrogant, elitist, plutocratic, insular, opaque, capricious, inbred, intellectually deficient, bureaucratic, and bewildered. These are surprising but not necessarily hurtful words for private philanthropy, because the people most connected to private foundations already know they are aristocratic and unaccountable and are rather pleased with the fact. These people serve on each other's boards, share in prestige's warm mutuality, and make certain that foundations are compliant with the values of the donor class. Moreover, this arrangement is careful to perpetuate itself. According to Stephen Viederman, former director of the Jessie Smith Noyes Foundation (a foundation that focuses on environmental and economic justice), replacements for departing foundation board members are almost always from the "world of top people" and are of the "same race, class, or occupational group as those who had served before."

In the end, the philanthropist's philosophy is this: We are virtuous because we have money. We are virtuous for giving away some of it each year. We give money only to the best causes that fall within our mission. We will tell you what the best causes are. We are under no obligation to tell you why the best causes are the best.

This may sound extreme, but it is not a new criticism. Parts of this critique have been in circulation since the first corporate philanthropic foundations were formed in the early twentieth century. Upon the formation of the Carnegie and Rockefeller foundations, there was fierce debate about their provenance, legality, and lack of accountability. Observers worried that non-tax-paying entities with massive resources and little accountability would be just another way for the wealthy to turn money into power.

The most dramatic problem facing capitalism for the last century has been its tendency to destroy the world in which it acts: the environmental crisis in all its manifestations. This crisis, particularly global warming, provides an urgent challenge for philanthropy, one that highlights long-simmering concerns about foundation giving. According to a report by the ClimateWorks Foundation, philanthropic giving to environmental organizations in 2023 ranged between $9.3 to $15.8 billion, most of which was directed toward mitigating, not eliminating, the causes of climate change. And it was only two percent of total foundation giving.

The response to this crisis in the United States has been the growth of the mainstream environmental movement, especially the Environmental Protection Agency and "Big Green": the Sierra Club, Greenpeace, the Nature Conservancy, the Natural Resource Defense Council, etc. But Big Green was not the pure consequence of an upswelling of popular generosity; it was also the creation of philanthropic, federal, and corporate gift giving.

The Natural Resources Defense Council was created by the Ford Foundation. The Pew Charitable Trusts created the National Environmental Fund. Pew itself was first endowed with money from the Sun Oil Company. At its inception, Pew's political views were deeply conservative. It advocated free markets and small government and funded the John Birch Society. These large environmental organizations are deeply dependent on federal and foundation support, and, accordingly, tend to take a soft line on economic and industrial reform. As Mark Dowie reported in his one-of-a-kind book *American Foundations*, Big Green organizations are "safe havens for foundation philanthropy, for their directors are sensitive to the economic orthodoxies that lead to the formation of foundations and careful not to do anything that might diminish the benefactor's endowment."

As with the Environmental Protection Agency, Big Green is not so much an enemy of industry as it is a self-regulator within it. In other words, the Sierra Club is not run by visionary rebels, it is upper management. Big Green does benefit the environment, but in no way is it hostile to the economic system that is the ultimate source of environmental destruction. As a consequence, a given industry may attack environmentalism when it interferes with its business, but big business as such is dependent on Big Green and will regularly replenish its coffers, never mind the occasional annoyance for an oil company that wants to spread its rigs and pipelines across delicate tundra.

The dependence of Big Green on philanthropic funds can also be nakedly political. Dowie reports in his book *Losing Ground* that in the early 1990s the Pew Charitable Trust entered the fray over public land forestry. Josh Reichert, Pew's environmental program officer, created a foundation coalition, the National Environmental Trust, to address forestry, among other issues. Once the money was handed out, large organizations like the Sierra Club fell in line, talked the talk, and took the funds. The problem was that this program was not allowed to consider a "zero cut" forestry position. The NET would concern itself only with moderating policy on behalf of corporate interests. Smaller, more principled organizations like the Native Forest Council were "left out in the cold." But Reichert was unapologetic. According to Dowie, "Reichert stipulated that no one advocating zero cut, criticizing corporations by name, or producing ads that did so would be eligible for membership in the forest coalition—or for funding."

Such restrictions are not rare. While there are over 50,000 foundations in the United States, there are only a few hundred funders in the Environmental Grantmakers Association (EGA). Environmental philanthropy is a small world. As one of my sources in the philanthropic world explained, blacklisting can take place quietly over wine: "I won't say anything bad about so-and-so, but I'll never fund him again." What's unspoken is "and you shouldn't fund him either."

This scenario is easy enough to imagine. The EGA was established in 1987 and funded by the Rockefeller Family Fund. Its one notable production is an annual fall retreat. In 2009, for example, the EGA membership gathered along the

Cook Inlet near Anchorage, Alaska. Among the enticements to participants was "a set of delicious pre- and post-retreat field trips." There are no agendas, minutes, or summaries of these meetings available to the public. Even the reports that the group creates ("Tracking the Field") are available in full only to members.

There is no reason for surprise if organizations like the EGA facilitate small but lethal talk over wine. This is how private philanthropy polices certain limits on what can be said—to ensure that their generosity doesn't become a weapon against them. As representatives of wealth, it is incumbent upon them to see to it that their work does not threaten the source of their wealth. And so when private philanthropy is asked to be more inclusive, to empower local environmental groups, to spend out endowments, it sounds as if it is being asked to become, in Nietzsche's words, "the will that wills its own destruction." As you would expect, foundations are bewildered by the suggestion and unwilling to do so.

The great paradox of environmental philanthropy is this: How do philanthropic institutions founded on wealth and privilege seek to address the root source of environmental destruction if that source is essentially the unbridled use of wealth and privilege? Ken Burns's 2009 film *The National Parks: America's Best Idea* provides an illuminating example of the paradox of self-interested altruism. If private philanthropy is to play a constructive role in addressing environmental destruction, it must come to terms with this internal contradiction. Unfortunately, more often than not, philanthropy's strategy is to pretend not to see the problem.

The most grotesque instance of this in *The National Parks* is Burns's introduction of John D. Rockefeller Jr. as one of the great philanthropic heroes in the establishment of our national parks. In 1928, Rockefeller stepped forward with five million dollars to save the Smoky Mountains. What isn't said is that Rockefeller's fortune came from his father's founding of the Standard Oil Trust, notorious for its use of private police for enforcing exploitive wages and murderous working conditions for its miners. Rockefeller's mining operations in Butte, Montana, turned the town into what it is to this day: one of the most toxic spots on Earth. Standard Oil created great hills of toxic slag, polluted over a hundred miles of the Silver Bow Creek (known to locals as "Shit Creek" for its sulfureous stench), and dug an open pit now filled with billions of gallons of acidic water. John D. Rockefeller Jr. continued his father's methods for profit extraction including the pitiless oppression of miners, culminating in the Ludlow Mining Massacre of 1914, only a few years before Rockefeller donated millions of dollars for the creation of Acadia National Park in Maine.

The failures of Burns's *The National Parks* are not solely failures of omission. There are also enormous failures of interpretation, or a refusal to interpret. For instance, Burns seems to assume that there is continuity between the work of the radical naturalist John Muir and the work of Stephen Mather, the New England philanthropist who was most responsible for recruiting the financial support of people like Rockefeller for the creation of national parks and for promoting the parks to the public. What Burns doesn't acknowledge is that Mather's work is at best a transformation of Muir's vision. Perhaps it can be said that every visionary needs a pragmatist to realize the vision, but Burns's film reveals a different sort of pattern, one that we see repeated in the work of environmental philanthropy today: First the visionary (Muir), then the millionaire philanthropist (Mather), and finally the whole thing is handed off to bureaucrats, who, for all their good works, can rarely be mistaken for naturalists. Most significantly, the role of heroic millionaire has evolved and is now institutionalized in philanthropic foundations. The pattern now: First the passionate work of grassroots activists; then the foundations come in; and finally the reign of data and the wisdom of bureaucracies through which nature becomes little more than a technical balancing act, an engineering problem on a global scale.

Perhaps *The National Parks* provides images of the beauty and even the spirituality of our national parks. The film is accompanied (as always with Burns) by spectral music that wells up symphonically and leaves its viewers with a feeling of national pride, aesthetic joy, and a sense that something magnificent has been accomplished. Nowhere, however, does the film risk the suggestion that the National Park system is also a deeply problematic idea because it puts a boundary on nature, beyond which we are free to be as destructive as we like. Drive across a park boundary and suddenly you're back in Petroleum World ("our national automobile slum," as James Howard Kunstler puts it). But this is not, obviously, the sort of argument that the corporate underwriters of *The National Parks* (which included General Motors and the Pew Charitable Trusts) would be willing to pay for.

In the end, what environmental philanthropy can be trusted to understand is not forest health, or climate change, or the imperatives of recycling. What it can be trusted to understand is the thing that gives it its privileges: its money. The foundation can be trusted above all to be duly diligent in the maintenance of its endowment. Unfortunately, managing how the endowment is invested often leads to conflicts with the stated social purpose of the foundation.

For example, one of the continuing controversies in the world of environmental philanthropy is the 95–5 question. Foundations are required to give away just 5 percent of their endowment each year. The other 95 percent is invested. But invested where? Environmentalists are particularly sensitive to this question because if the money is invested in companies that continue to pollute and destroy the environment, you have a very disturbing reality. The 5 percent does theoretical good while 95 percent does demonstrable bad: chasing profits in environmentally destructive ways.

This issue came to a head in 2007 when an investigation by the *Los Angeles Times* into the investment practices of foundations concluded that the Gates Foundation funded a polio vaccination clinic in Ebocha, Nigeria, in the shadow of a giant petroleum processing plant in which the Gates Foundation was invested. The *Los Angeles Times* report states:

> But polio is not the only threat Justice [a Nigerian child] faces. Almost since birth, he has had respiratory trouble. His neighbors call it "the cough." People blame fumes and soot spewing from flames that tower 300 feet into the air over a nearby oil plant. It is owned by the Italian petroleum giant Eni, whose investors include the Bill & Melinda Gates Foundation.

Despite intense criticism at the time, the Gates Foundation did not change course. An investigation of the foundation's tax return for 2013 performed by *The Guardian* revealed that it held $1.4 billion of investment in fossil fuel companies including British Petroleum and Anadarko Petroleum (which was forced to pay $5 billion in environmental cleanup charges). These outsized investments cut against the grain, to put it mildly, of Bill Gates's claim that "The long-term threat [of climate change] is so serious that the world needs to move much more aggressively—right now—to develop energy sources that are cheaper, can deliver on demand, and emit zero carbon dioxide."

This is a conflict to which environmentalism is especially sensitive, and foundations ought to be. And yet, incredibly, the Gates Foundation chose to deny that the conflict is a conflict. As chief executive Patty Stonesifer said in 2007: "It would be naïve to think that changing the foundation's investment policy could stop the human suffering blamed on the practices of companies in which it invests billions of dollars." This is tantamount to saying that if the Gates Foundation didn't invest in Eni's profitable venture someone else would. We've seen this sort of argument before, though it usually comes from private companies. For example, British Petroleum defended its role in the exportation of Alberta tar sands by saying: "These are resources that would have been developed anyway." BP perhaps feels that it is protecting profits for its shareholders, but what shareholder is the Gates Foundation protecting? If it must continue to invest in Eni, why doesn't the Gates Foundation file a stockholder resolution protesting Eni's methods? The dark irony is that the Gates Foundation saves Nigerians from polio now, but it is morally indifferent to the lung diseases that will kill them later.

The simple fact is that most foundation boards don't know if their investments and their missions align. When pushed on the matter, most foundations respond as the Gates Foundation did: Investments are the foundation's private concern and no business of ours. But the problem remains, when environmental organizations receive funding, what confidence can they have that the origin of this happy money isn't in environmentally destructive business practices?

Of course, from an environmentalist's perspective the preservation of a foundation's endowment is a much less pressing matter than the facts on the ground, especially if that fact is climate change. Left to itself, industry is not going to do anything about a warming Earth. In fact, it is most likely to make matters worse. As Mark Bittman wrote in a penetrating opinion essay for *The New York Times*, in the middle of a historic drought that threatens the future of California, too much of the agriculture industry is "mining water as they would copper: When it runs out, they'll find new ways to make money."

Ideally, private philanthropy would play an aggressive role in countering the logic of exploitation for short-term profit, even if that means digging deeper into endowments. But that does not seem to be what's happening. Most foundations still give away only five percent of their endowment each year, the legal minimum. But if climate change must be successfully addressed within the next decade, if it's really the critical moral issue of our time, or any time, why spend only five percent? For a simple reason: Spending five percent annually will allow the foundation to do its work into eternity. Sadly, a world without a livable climate is easier for the philanthropist to imagine than a world without the family foundation. Sadder still, philanthropy's unwillingness to spend and act more aggressively makes it too much like the water gluttons of California, for whom self-interest outrivals all other concerns. This will only get worse as foundations tailor their giving to the ideological constraints of the Far Right: Witness the Gates Foundation's unceremonious dumping of the left-leaning Arabella Advisors network of non-profit organizations in 2025.

The good news is that there are many people who understand the problem and are beginning to push for change in the priorities of corporate foundations. In 2014, one-hundred-and-sixty leading environmentalists from forty-six countries called on foundations and philanthropists to use their endowments to turn the tide on global warming. "We, 160 winners of the world's environmental prizes, call on foundations and philanthropists everywhere to deploy their endowments immediately in the effort to save civilization. The world's philanthropic foundations, given the scale of their endowments, hold the power to trigger a survival reflex in society." And in a 2025 article in *Inside Philanthropy*, David Callahan provides an overview of major gift-giving coming out of finance. Included in this overview are former Secretary of the Treasury Henry Paulson and Julian Robertson, "the Wizard of Wall Street." Callahan observes that Wall Street's winners would be well advised to be attentive to climate change because their place of business, Wall Street, is likely to be underwater soon if they aren't.

Business is not opposed in principle to morality, but

morality is always, as Robert Heilbroner thought, an antieconomic impulse. The problem for capitalism is how to manage morality so that its anti-economic effects are minimal. Properly handled, morality could become a market player (cap-and-trade schemes, for example). Unfortunately, thanks to these foundations, environmentalism's moral impulse is now indistinguishable from the delicate balancing act that is the national economy: both are subject to the calculus of "cost–benefit."

The greatest moral problem for environmental philanthropy is that it doesn't have what the theologian Paul Tillich called an "ultimate concern." The movement at present has finite campaigns, like mercury levels in fish or parts-per-million of greenhouse gases, but it has no ultimate concern. To have an ultimate concern would mean that environmentalism commits itself to an ideal and knows exactly what it means by that commitment. Environmental philanthropy makes no existential wagers of this sort.

If environmental philanthropy were to discover its own sense of moral purpose, it would find itself in a frightening new context. To cut a deal in keeping with the "best practices" of a bureaucracy is one thing. But to cut a deal that violates your own ultimate concerns is quite another. For Tillich, sin is whatever separates us from our ultimate concerns. But "no worries," as we say these days, American philanthropy is there to make sure our decisions are pragmatic in the vulgar sense: They put off the final day when all their moral shuffling comes to a conclusion and their benevolence is shown to be only a subtle form of malice.

## TECHNICALLY, IT'S ENSHITTIFICATION

> "How did you go bankrupt?" Bill asked.
>
> "Two ways," Mike said. "Gradually and then suddenly."
>
> —Ernest Hemingway, *The Sun Also Rises*

Philanthropy is not the only form that capitalism's perverse virtue signaling takes. Corporations look to enhance their brands by presenting themselves as a force for good through mottos like Google's "Don't be evil"; its parent company Alpha's "Do the right thing"; Amazon's "Delivering Smiles"; Microsoft's "Innovate, Integrate, Inspire"; or Apple's "Think Different." The mottos change as frequently as the products they hope to sell, but they have always been more about market positioning than moral presence. Their claims to upright moral bearing have been "enshittified." For example, Google has betrayed its original sense of purpose through alleged mass surveillance, manipulating search engine results, censoring political content, manipulating public opinion, and generally behaving like what it is: an amoral monopolist. And yet, even though Google's original motto is now laughable, it still makes claim to virtue through programs like "Search Inside Yourself" (SIY), which until recently sought to join corporate culture to a vaguely Buddhist pursuit of "emotional intelligence." Predictably, in 2022 SIY became SIY Global, a for-profit corporation whose stated purpose is to "integrate social and emotional intelligence skills into work culture."

Of course, producers of consumer goods have always advertised their product's virtues for competitive advantage. But because tech capitalism was trying to sell something that had not previously existed, it appealed to the self-identity of its target market: well-educated, affluent, and ethically conscious people who were the moral inheritors of 1960s counterculture. But over time, in a process of "enshittification," companies left moral substance behind, confident that whether because of habit, addiction, or exhaustion their customers would not be lost. The term was invented by Cory Doctorow who commented

> Platforms go bad in this very typical way. First, they're good to end users, and they find a way to lock those end users in. And then once the end users are locked into the Roach Motel—users check in, but they don't check out—they make things a little worse for those end users, knowing that they can't readily leave.

Tech's ethical commitments declined gradually, then went suddenly bankrupt, leaving it morally unbound and therefore free to gather at Donald Trump's narcissistic festivities, wallets open.

Apple founder Steve Jobs's first business insight was that he could associate Apple's products with cultural icons of opposition—like Bob Dylan, John Lennon, and the Buddha—to create a market for personal computing. In its early years, Apple presented itself as a countercultural force opposed to big, soulless IBM. Unlike IBM, soulful Apple used the mystique of Zen to create a technological spiritualism. The clean, unadorned style of Apple's products adopted the stark simplicity of Zen art and calligraphy. But the Zen influence did not stop with design. As Brett T. Robinson, author of *Appletopia*, has commented approvingly, "The iconic iPod campaign shows dancers in shadow form, connoting the bodiless, spiritual quality of being immersed in music." For Steve Jobs, the computer was a spiritual liberator—or so he wanted us to believe. This strategy was so successful that even IBM followed suit with its "Smiling Mind" app to introduce its workers to meditation and "mental wellbeing and the habits to thrive."

But, of course, Apple's claim that it is informed by Buddhist values attracts a lot more skepticism in the present than it did in the 1990s. Now it seems more credible to say that Apple was merely the first manufacturer to use Buddhism to brand its products. These days, Buddha branding has created the oxymoron of a Buddhist consumerism. There is today an array of Buddha-branded products and programs that coopt an otherwise antagonistic discourse, just as the 1960s counterculture was coopted by Madison Avenue in what Thomas Frank has called the great "conquest of cool."

Aaron Sorkin and Danny Boyle's 2015 movie *Steve Jobs* is a critical examination of a man whose persona drove the development, both early and late, of Silicon Valley and its high-tech industries. The movie would have us believe that it is a candid examination of this "flawed genius," and it does put a harsh light on the man's megalomania, duplicity, and lack of compassion. What *Steve Jobs* is critical of—Jobs's relationship to family and friends, especially to his daughter Lisa and Apple co-founder Steve Wozniak—is rendered through a long, painful-to-endure series of quarrels. There are better stories; this is soap opera.

No plot drives the movie. It is structured instead through Apple's public product launches. In three acts, these launches are joined to backstage quarrels, while Jobs shuttles between the two spaces and between two very different versions of himself. The movie has the feel of a long and ill-tempered family spat. Its aesthetic is the theater of the petty and the unpleasant. *Steve Jobs* is scandal, is tabloid fodder (even if the tabloid is *The New York Times*), but it is not serious.

Which is a way of saying that this movie about the dishonesty of Jobs is itself dishonest. It is true that for millions of offended admirers, the Steve Jobs image emerges with blemishes that will now become part of the way he is remembered. His cultish admirers can't be happy about that. On the other hand, the Apple mythology emerges unscathed, and that must offer tremendous consolation to the tech industry. So, while the world argues about just how bad Jobs was as a husband, father, and friend, his narrative about the meaning of Apple remains sublime. The film's conclusion is shameless in its invocation of Dylan, Einstein, Gandhi, and John Lennon. (The original Apple—the Apple that Apple computers replaced—was the Beatles' Apple Records, where artists didn't "have to go on their knees in somebody's office," as Lennon explained.) Whatever Jobs's personal flaws, Apple's famously personal products are still about "think different;" they represent rebellion commodified, and that is still tremendously useful for the tech industry's self-promotion.

Sorkin and Boyle share Jobs's hubris. In a critical scene in the film, just as Jobs is leaving his dressing room for the stage, Joanna Hoffman (played by Kate Winslet) encourages him, saying, "Now go out there and put a dent in the universe." Packed into this statement is an attitude and even a worldview, endorsed uncritically by the film, that says, among other things: The universe is here for us to put dents in, and creating these dents provides not only technological innovation but moral progress, an unqualified good. Jobs was a master at selling this evangelical view of technology.

Were they serious, Sorkin and Boyle would have looked

more carefully at these dents. Yes, Jobs admired the simplicity and clarity of the Buddhist temples and gardens he visited in Japan, but everything else about his company functioned through *dukkha*, suffering: Apple's monopolistic business practices, its indifference to labor standards at "iPhone City," Foxconn's notorious Zhengzhou factory, its evasion of business taxes through offshore shell companies, and its criminal rigging of self-enriching "back-dated stock options" for its executives. None of this finds a place in Sorkin and Boyle's movie. We are asked to be content with whatever seriousness can be found in a melodrama about a wealthy but selfish father abandoning his daughter and betraying his friends. Meanwhile, the fact that the Buddha has been rendered a mere shill for iPhones passes without comment.

The criticism in *Steve Jobs* is the criticism of no criticism.

Happily, there are compelling examples of how resistant culture can un-tell the stories of the dominant culture and begin to tell its own. Alexandra Pelosi's 2015 documentary *San Francisco 2.0* examines the tech industry's hostile takeover of San Francisco. Tech stands accused of selling the city to its employees as a perk (what tech-savvy urban hipster wants to live in suburban Cupertino?). Pelosi's film suggests that San Francisco has become one vast gated community.

She asks two questions: How do the dot-com corporations and startups understand what they are doing in San

Francisco and the South Bay? And how do the longtime residents of San Francisco experience the arrival of the techies? Then she lets the people involved tell their stories.

The tech bros are not unsympathetic. They're smart, excited about what they're doing, and just as open to new ideas as they are reputed to be. You'd say that there is something anarchistic about them if it weren't an anarchism swimming in vast pools of venture capital. They are by all appearances having fun, enjoying both their work and each other, but they are really, really detached from what their presence means for the people living in a city with its own important history. Pelosi's film reveals them as charming and bright but lacking in sympathetic imagination—the ability to imagine what it's like to be someone other than yourself.

The techies live in a youth bubble. It is implausible to them that among the "old people" they are replacing are the artists, poets, bohemians, and generally, as Jobs would put it, the "different" who once thrived in The City. The arrival of the techies in San Francisco, now a weird sort of bedroom community for Silicon Valley, makes literal the old Firesign Theater joke about the Trail of Tears Golf Course: "We're moving them out to make room for you!"

And yet when the youngsters are confronted with these criticisms, they seem impatient, as if they don't quite see why they should have to bother about local issues when they have more important things to do, things that Steve

Jobs understood better than anyone before or since—they are making people rich and they are "creating the future." Isn't that enough?

The ancients called this attitude "hubris" or pride. And you know what pride cometh before, literally in the case of San Francisco's Millennium Tower next door to the Salesforce Office Tower, the largest office space in San Francisco. The office tower is emptying, but the fate of the Millennium is worse. It is sinking, threatening to topple, and shedding massive windowpanes on the pedestrians below.

On the other hand, the older residents of The City's once diverse neighborhoods are, not surprisingly, bitter. And for good reasons: gays are being priced out of the Castro, Hispanics are being priced out of the Mission, African Americans are simply being physically displaced as their homes are torn down in Hunters Point, making room for condominiums at the Hunters Point Shipyard Development. But where do art, music, culture, and affordable housing fit in this scheme?

Pelosi's film is not only a "bad review" of the tech bros who took over San Francisco, it is also an act of resistance. It cuts across the grain of the heroic story that tech has tried to tell about itself. What Pelosi reminds us about is the once familiar fact of urban community, its neighborhoods and villages. "This was," she says. She allows us to hear the human voices that once enlivened our cities. Just knowing that those voices once lived leads us to imagine that they might thrive again. Unlike Stefan Zweig's *The World of Yesterday*, Pelosi's film leads us forward to Nietzsche's "next joyful deed."

## MANAGING DESPAIR: A THEORY OF LIBERALISM

> Free action is to live in the present society as though it were a natural society.
>
> —Paul Goodman, *The May Pamphlet*

After a national electoral beat down such as Democrats suffered in 2024, there is always handwringing over the future of liberalism. The anxiety behind this handwringing is, obviously, the possibility that liberalism might not have a future, that this time the conservatives have really done it, they have succeeded in returning to 1880.

The robber barons . . . they're back! (As if they ever left.)

The liberal response to this anxiety is always to compromise the hell out of what you had claimed were your values, hope the Republicans overreach, and try to win at the polls in the next election cycle. What's pathetic about this is that no need is felt for real self-analysis. What is liberalism, after all? Is it something that deserves a future? I would claim that a large part of the problem of liberalism is that it doesn't know itself. I propose to help it understand itself even if self-understanding turns out to be something it wishes it didn't have. I propose to tell a better story about liberalism.

An understanding of liberalism begins with the recognition that it is not the creation of a vast popular movement rooted in the labor struggles of the 1880s through the 1930s. Working people did not create liberalism. The truth is that what we know as liberalism is the creation of an oligarchy (or the ruling class, or the masters, or rich people, or the boss, if any of those terms satisfy you, and I wouldn't blame you if they didn't). I prefer the term oligarch because it reminds us that our problem with entrenched power is not so different from what the Greeks and Romans knew: The rule of a small number of people of unwholesome wealth who have co-opted the political state through measures both violent and rhetorically facile.

What the oligarchy was forced to acknowledge between 1880 and 1930—forced not by the powerful opposition of "the people" but by a stark reality of its own making—was that their proud creation, laissez-faire capitalism, had magnificently imploded. Beginning with the Great Depression of 1873 (which lasted nearly twenty years in some parts of the country), followed by the Depression of 1893, then 1896, and culminating with the stock market crash of 1929, capitalism died. It dug itself a very deep hole and threw itself in. Left to its own devices, capitalism had no idea how to restore markets or, for God's scary sake, to resist all those workers with their awful slogans, like "Kickin' Ass for the Working Class."

The failure of capitalism was a problem for oligarchs because they still depended on the use of property and the exploitation of labor markets for the continued maintenance of their wealth and status. There was no path back to the rentier class for them. So, the first coherent social liberalism, what we call the New Deal, came forward and in essence created a new social and economic system more or less from scratch. The implementation of this system saved large portions of capitalist property, production, and finance, but at the same time it forced the capitalist to move forward in cooperation with Big Government and Big Labor. From that point forward, we no longer had a free market economy, nor was it a planned economy. What we had was a negotiated economy. The 2009 bailout of the auto industry, accomplished with the full participation of corporate boards, federal government, and the United Auto Workers, was the most recent example of the strategic cooperation that has defined our economy since the 1930s.

In other words: Fare thee well, titans of industry! Come on down, tinhorn regulators! The best description of this novel economic order is in the work of the great American economist John Kenneth Galbraith. Galbraith called the edifice created by the New Deal a "techno-structure."

The term New Deal—with its implication of greater fairness for working people, a better deal for them—is misleading. The more accurate term would be the New System. If working people were better off under the New System, it was incidental, something conceded grudgingly. The rapacious destruction of unionism over the last fifty years is a much better measure of how the oligarchy has always felt about working people. The oligarchs still believe that people should be paid as little as possible—ideally no more than is necessary for the reproduction of the labor supply. The oligarch's concern for labor is roughly what the factory trawler's concern is for cod: leave a "sustainable" population necessary to produce next year's catch. But as the collapse of the Atlantic cod fisheries showed in the 1990s, and growing income inequality has shown more recently, oligarchs are not particularly good at self-limiting. They need the help of liberal managers who can claim to have the interests of the cod and the people who catch them at heart.

Galbraith argued that after 1935 neo-classical market economics was no longer a "description of reality." The new reality is a system removed from the traditional workings of market supply and demand. The New System limited the authority of commerce and even directed the desires of the consumer (through the creation of "artificial needs," as Galbraith expressed it in *The Affluent Society*). In this new arrangement, no one possessed power except the system itself. The political state became the executive committee of the New System, and its ultimate function, realized through a bewildering panoply of code and regulation applied to every facet of economic life, was to maintain stability for the whole ungainly edifice by balancing the interests of the three primary players. Through the rise of the modern state-regulated corporate organization, antitrust laws became irrelevant because, as Galbraith thought, "a government cannot proclaim half of the economic system illegal." In short, the government itself became a partner to monopoly and so did labor.

This precocious truth has been made abundantly clear in the era of Big Tech in which monopolists like Microsoft and Google become not only "too big to fail" but "too big to mess with." In theory, monopolies are illegal, but in fact the New System was dependent on them. Stranger yet, monopolies like the tech Big Five—Alphabet, Amazon, Apple, Meta, and Microsoft—are now becoming what we once feared: a planned economy. Education, media, social communication, manufacturing, utilities, marketing, *space travel!* . . ., who needs the Politburo when we have Jeff Bezos?

Beyond this Herculean project of inventing a new kind of economy out of the smoldering remains of the last, liberalism's ongoing job title has been designated worrier. Its job description is to manage despair. The despair that it is best known for managing is the despair of labor. Just as Smith, Malthus, and Marx understood, the capitalist market system is as much a scheme for making poverty as it is a scheme for making prosperity. This despair is a cause worthy of worry because enough poor people with nothing to do but go hungry creates an environment conducive to rebellion, whether by slave, peasant, or worker. And so we have seen liberal worriers like Nancy Pelosi explain in

2017 that, "We're capitalists, and that's just the way it is." But then qualify her assertion by saying that, yes, capitalism is not adequately responding to income inequality.

In the New Deal era, managing despair meant borrowing extensively from a socialist program for reform. Between 1930 and 1975, the New System created laws protecting the right of workers to organize and bargain collectively, and it provided social legislation to protect citizens against poverty, old age, racism, and, with Richard Nixon's creation of the EPA in 1970, the destruction of the environment. It even borrowed from Marx. It is enlightening to read the last pages of *The Communist Manifesto* where Marx and Engels lay out the rudiments for a future communist society. Among their recommendations are free universal public education, a graduated income tax, limits on inheritance, the centralization of credit in a national bank, and the centralization of the means of communication and transportation. All of these things are now a familiar part of the American economic bargain, however much the political Right now works to destroy them.

But there was a concrete benefit for oligarchs in managing the despair of working people: It made revolution much less likely. The oligarchs could stop worrying about the Wobblies, and they didn't have to mobilize their private goon squads every time the miners went on strike, a real plus for public relations.

The second despair that liberalism manages is the despair of the oligarchy itself when it is made victim to the natural destructiveness and instability of capitalist markets. The oligarchy needs this liberal managing because the natural logic of the capitalist is this: "People may suffer, a world of animals may go extinct, wars may rage, the corpses may pile high, the climate may come to look like something designed to murder dinosaurs, but I bet that, in spite of all this, I will profit. In fact, I look forward to the challenge. My very survival will be the mark of my superiority and will justify my privileges, especially my exemption from suffering."

Friends, I give you Elon Musk.

For capitalism, the ignominious, whining life that it endures when run through liberal regulation is shameful. Liberalism is death with a whimper. Conservative oligarchs and their minions want to live capitalism "all in." They reserve for themselves the right to go out with a bang, taking everything with them if that's the way it works out. So be it! They will be all-conquering, or they will be nothing at all.

Friends, I give you Donald Trump.

Should someone ask why oligarchs are allowed to thrive while people go hungry and the planet burns, they will simply turn on their smartphones and open their electronic wallets. See? A thousand, a million, a billion, a godzillion. Now do you get it? As Chico Marx said while bidding in the auction scene in the movie *Cocoanuts*, "I got plenty numbers."

We live in an ever-warmer haze of our own waste. Animal species fall at our feet like mysteriously dying birds. Oil washes in clots upon our beaches as if it were the gore of a distant corpse. So bad is the situation that even earthquakes, floods, and the eruption of volcanoes seem to comment on our guilt, as if the gods were making a last desperate attempt to gain our attention.

Wealth will be under no obligation to make sense in relation to the impoverished and frightening hordes swarming in the dystopic hinterlands, the food deserts, the parched valleys where lettuce once grew. Bitcoin and other digital currencies will have no objective value, not in gold, not in collateral, and certainly not in the good faith and credit of the nation-state—which is now, literally, a bit player. But, then, virtual money is nothing new. Money has always been virtual, a fantasy legitimating the relationship between affluence and despair.

Is this where evolution has been heading for the last two million years? These self-destructive and vainglorious creatures are the fittest? The most dominant members of the most dominant species in the long history of life on earth behaving like a perverse crow that gathers into its nest a treasure of shiny bottle caps, shreds of aluminum foil, a glass earring . . . and then shits on it? If so, then evolution may be a scientific fact, but it is a very bad idea.

# LIVE BETTER STORIES

A string of facts, however well attested, has no power to correct or dislodge a powerful story. The only thing that can displace a story is a story. —George Monbiot

## CULT AND CULTURE

> A populace that is chloroformed day and night by TV stations like Fox News could do with inoculation by poetry. Obviously, poetry can't be administered like an injection, but it does constitute a boost to the capacity for discrimination and resistance. —**Seamus Heaney**

Once we have gained distance from our masters' stories—philanthropy, virtuous corporations, liberal managers of despair—it is possible to tell and live through our own stories, making ourselves useless to purposes other than our own.

Although our stories must begin with critique, ultimately we will turn to the arts because the fundamental question that art asks is: "After having experienced this poem, this song, this painting, can you return to the world you have known till this moment? Or has the work shown you that you must change your life?" That question is the substance of great art's greatness. That question is art's human purpose.

Art is part of a larger contestation put forward by what is "eccentric," ex-centric, outside of the shrinking circle into which we are born, the perimeter that tells us what will be allowed, what is acceptable—following the law of the social norm. LGBTQ communities have shown us the importance of the ex-centric; witness Gay Pride Parades and their attendant follies. Calmer and less colorful but no less important are local organic farms, farmers' markets, and DIY craft shows. Add to these the ongoing independent literary press movement, alternative media like *CounterPunch*, *Jacobin*, and *Truthout*, and mutual aid societies. All of this is gladly ex-centric and shares art's longing for what is life-giving.

But, as you will know, there are contrary forces at work. The arts and the humanities are being relegated to the vast category of the irrelevant. This is not news, but the presentation of this process of erosion in the mainstream media is mostly abstract and disengaged. The executive branch did this; the courts said that; everything was resolved through huge sums of money. What's missing in these accounts is the human cruelty implicit within an ongoing technocratic betrayal.

Contrary to what the media would have us believe, culture is not merely the customs of a place, its language, religion, and cuisine. Nor is culture merely the movies, the music, the Internet of Things, nor the rest of capitalist life's fabulously stippled frou-frous. These are very static ways of thinking about culture. Properly understood, culture is a process of becoming. As Sigmund Freud wrote, culture is the act of "replacing what is unconscious with what is conscious." A cult is unconscious. It simply does what it has always done. It follows instructions. Culture, on the other hand, brings to awareness the damage—the repression, irrationality, violence, ugliness, injustice, and tragedy—imposed by the cult. In this sense, culture is enlightenment.

And in this sense . . . the United States is a cult, a long-enduring truth made inescapable in the Trump era. A cult without culture is not capable of Freud's enlightenment. It has only its crude and cruel version of eternity: "This is how we do this, we have always done it this way, we will always do it this way, this is not negotiable, it is not worth thinking about let alone talking about, it just is, and, by the way, shut up or else." And so, if you are in Saudi Arabia, do not write blogs seeking to open a frank discussion of Islam or you will go to jail. A very unpleasant jail, and jailers with whips for lashing. And if you're in Thailand, do not insult the king or even his mongrel pet dog or you will go to jail. A very unpleasant jail, and "et cetera, et cetera, and so forth," as a fictional King of Siam once put it. The cult enforces what is to be done through constant reference to what has already been done. And, as we know, it is deadly serious about its enforcement responsibilities. Disgracefully, these foreign outrages are not foreign on our shores, especially if you are an immigrant and are confronted by the cult of "America First."

As with psychoanalysis, the dialectic between cult and culture is "interminable." That is, analysis is not about achieving a cure, or establishing good mental health, or fixing anything. For Freud, there is no such thing as health. That is because the neurotic symptom is not the sign of an illness. In fact, neurotics are loyal to their symptoms, and for the same reason that a Texan is loyal to the NRA: They believe this loyalty is deserved, honorable, and necessary for self-preservation. Freud illustrates this peculiarity with a revealing anecdote in his monumental *Introductory Lectures on Psychoanalysis*:

> An Arab was riding a camel along a narrow path cut in the steep face of a mountain. At a turn in the path he suddenly found himself face-to-face with a lion, which prepared to make a spring. He saw no way out: on one side a perpendicular cliff and on the other a precipice; retreat or flight weren't possible. He gave himself up for lost. But the animal thought otherwise. He took one leap with his rider into the abyss—and the lion was left in the lurch.

The camel's decision to avoid the jaws of the lion by jumping off a cliff is the neurotic symptom. It is an attempt at self-preservation through self-destruction. The neurosis itself is nothing in particular, certainly not an "illness." It is merely the perverse assumption by patients that they can be saved through doing things that are suicidal. If, for example, the problem (or lion) is gun violence, the neurotic remedy is to bring more guns into our homes in the name of self-defense. If the problem is industrial capitalism's destruction of the natural world, the best response is to give it more "self-correcting" freedom from EPA regulation. Of course, this is perfectly "stupid." Freud's practice merely attempts to make the patient aware of the stupidity. He preferred an honorable confrontation with the lion, which is to say, an honorable confrontation with our stupidities. And so should we.

Freud's solution for this quandary is awareness, coming to understand that the threat doesn't exist in the way we imagine that it does, and seeing that our reaction to the perceived threat is self-destructive. Suddenly the world is new because it now allows for the possibility of possibilities beyond living in a cult as a neurotic. With the lion out of the way, a therapeutic solution offers itself: Create a different world that doesn't require you to jump off a cliff. Instead of being crazy, create a world that is more conducive to organic thriving. Freud's answer to the lion was to walk through it like the apparition (or delusion) it is, and, on the other side, to create something different. Because we should be free to create a world of Otherwise.

For Freud, we arrive at this world-beyond-the-lion through what he called "sublimation," redirecting self-destructive energy toward creativity, toward artful living.

## THE END OF THE LIBERAL ARTS DREAM

> Because irony knows no limits and recognizes an easy mark when it sees one, it is certain that the sixties generation—raised on revolution and yearning ... for its return—will find, when revolution does return, that they are the ones to be overthrown.
>
> —"Four Theses on the Fate of the Sixties," from *The Idea of Home*, 1992

Our world is the opposite of artful and therefore the opposite of therapeutic. Rather, it continues what the Freudian psycho-theorist Karen Horney called "the neurotic personality of our time." Our neurosis insists that everything outside of us is potentially a threat of some kind—whether economic, military, or social—and that the only way to confront that threat is through strength and competition or, in other words, through violence variously expressed, even when that violence is self-destructive, as in the case of Freud's camel.

Until recently, universities offered another path: a distinctive form of community, a culture that reasoned, intuited, and was generally open to new conclusions. In the university we could spend a few years learning what seemed to us worthy of knowing. Students could walk away from the neurotic assumptions of the general culture and study, as I did, Aristotle's *Nicomachean Ethics*, of all unlikely things.

In both the public and private sectors, the corporate university has been slowly growing for many years, but it has now become more brazen in its destructive tendencies. For an example that is close to me personally, the Board of Trustees at Illinois Wesleyan University (IWU) in Bloomington, Illinois, announced in May of 2020 that it was eliminating many long-established programs, all of which were in the liberal arts and social sciences. I say this is personal because my wife, Georganne Rundblad, taught sociology at Wesleyan for twenty-five years, and many of the faculty there were among our friends.

Without the consent of the faculty, the Board of Trustees sent pre-termination letters to twenty-five professors and instructional staff in philosophy, anthropology, music, foreign languages, sociology, art, and religion—in total, about a quarter of IWU's faculty. A liberal arts university without philosophers is a contradiction in terms, but a Wesleyan university without a department of religion is an exercise in self-mockery. No doubt, IWU will continue to claim that its "primary focus" is in "opening students' minds," but the college of business will have to do most of the opening. As UK Education Secretary Charles Clarke put it all too clearly, education should be about "harnessing knowledge to wealth creation."

Those departments that were not eliminated were said to need "transformation." Provost Mark Brodl told faculty member Scott Sheridan that "philosophy will support business and accounting, computer science and data science." In another example of what Julien Benda called the *trahison des clercs*, university president Georgia Nugent (a classicist by training) said that the department of art will "move more in the direction of art and design," including graphic design and product design. In other words, before the arts can transform students, commerce will first transform the arts. Andy Warhol saw it coming: Art is a can of soup.

Of course, there's no reason to think that this is the end of the transformations, these latest shudders of what Bill Readings called "the university in ruins." (Readings: "The contemporary University is busily transforming itself from an ideological arm of the state into a bureaucratically organized and relatively autonomous consumer-oriented corporation.") Remaining faculty can't sleep comfortably while wondering who and what will be cut next, a year from now, five years or ten. University boards can wait—they've been waiting patiently for fifty years. For fifty years American universities have moved toward a sense of mission that only a businessman can recognize, respect, and, most importantly, donate money to. It is as if private equity is swooping in and downsizing zombie assets. Eventually there will be mergers and acquisitions, which will mean fewer universities and colleges more centrally located.

But a university that doesn't recognize the value of the liberal arts shouldn't transform anything. It should shut its doors, fold it all up. It's better than becoming what Illinois Wesleyan has become: a watery version of the Wharton School of Business. To call what remains a university is not even "truthy," it's mendacious.

Wesleyan trustees felt no need to provide a rationale for their actions beyond the crude idea that the affected programs were not cost-efficient and that financial exigency threatened them in the near future—never mind the university's $200 million endowment. They offered no educational reasons for the changes, and no argument for how the changes were consistent with the values of the institution. Like the bandits in John Huston's *The Treasure of the Sierra Madre*, they said, "Reasons? We don't need no stinking reasons."

The feelings of the Illinois Wesleyan faculty and alums were raw at the time because they felt, rightfully, betrayed. One member of the IWU Alumni for the Liberal Arts, Molly McLay, wrote to me:

> I am infuriated by the lack of humanity and empathy in this process. Most of my professional work revolves around understanding, responding to, and preventing trauma. I truly think this experience at IWU has been a collective trauma.

Affirming McLay's thought, Scott Sheridan, a professor of French and Italian, commented:

> I feel like I'm just caught in the middle of an administration that has lost its bearings, that is changing the rules on me late in my career. I've bought into the ivory tower model, I've done everything asked of me, and

> now when the economy has tanked, Covid is blazing, higher ed is collapsing, and the University has damaged my professional reputation, I find myself completely cast aside, looking at the necessity not only to retool my professional objectives but to rethink my life.

Big Tech's infamous slogan, "Move fast and break things," is really a dressed-up form of "creative destruction," what Joseph Schumpeter called "the essential fact about capitalism" in his 1942 book *Capitalism, Socialism, and Democracy*. And Schumpeter was only civilizing the old Wall Street saw attributed to Baron Rothschild, "Buy when there's blood in the streets, even if the blood is your own." With their corporate boards, American universities now think the same thing, which a bloodied Professor Sheridan has learned to his dismay. Trustees, indeed!

Rudy H. Fichtenbaum, president of the American Association of University Professors, has described the situation simply:

> Replace full-time faculty protected by tenure with just-in-time trainers—part-time faculty who rightly fear losing their jobs if they question the dictates of the growing army of administrators that supervises them—and, voilà! The faculty no longer control the curriculum; the professional administrators puppeted by corporate interests do.

The motto over Wesleyan's portal should no longer be "Scientia et Sapientia," knowledge and wisdom. I propose that it should read like a legend over an AI version of Dante's Inferno: "No Admittance Except on Business."

After the Second World War, there was an enormous investment in public education. For the first time under the New System, the children of the working class had an opportunity to study subjects, like literature, that were formerly the privilege of the children of the affluent. We studied the humanities and the social sciences and in so doing found ways to critique and resist American business culture and its murderous inequalities. Many of the protestors of the present—marching with Black Lives Matter, or against gender bigotry, or against genocide in Gaza, or against the world as organized for the benefit of oil companies—honed their intellectual chops in universities, by taking courses like Professor Rundblad's "Sex and Gender in Society" or "Race and Ethnic Relations."

But our masters have been paying attention, and they have seen clearly and correctly: For most students, going to college was and remains a liberalizing experience. Our plutocrat masters concluded, "So this is what happens when you let the working class and minorities go to college. They study things of no value to us, and they learn to hate us."

As a consequence, slowly, decade after decade, humanities departments were starved and students were put in debt. Meanwhile, the wealthy came to the rescue and became university trustees. In these fallen days, the ideal trustee is someone who has money or knows people with money, ideally both. (The chair of Wesleyan's Board of Trustees is Timothy Szerlong, former president of worldwide field operations at CNA Financial Corporation.)

The ultimate benefit of all this for our oligarchs is a new but very powerful form of social regimentation. Their message to students: "If you want a job, you will study what we want you to study, or else you will live in debt." We could call this naked coercion, but for students it is their first adult taste of American Un-freedom.

In 1969, the year before I entered the University of San Francisco, I was working at a McDonalds in the East Bay. The franchise owner liked me and offered me a scholarship to McDonald's Hamburger University in Chicago. I laughed. I shouldn't have.

## THE LATE WORD

Since the corporate university has decided that its students have no need of the arts and humanities, it is worth remembering that for most of the last two centuries art and its criticism have thrived outside of academies, in part because artists have long suspected that the academy was not a flourishing place. They couldn't pursue their muses there, wherever they might lead. Henri de Toulouse-Lautrec, Claude Debussy, Friedrich Nietzsche, Paul Cézanne, Gertrude Stein, Egon Schiele, and most other nineteenth-

and twentieth-century artists worthy of memory, as well as art critics like Denis Diderot (painting), Baudelaire (music), Coleridge (poetry), and John Berger (any and everything), all had antagonistic relationships with the rules for proper art-making laid down by the academy. Most of these figures were either born into wealth, or otherwise scraped by writing for journals and living in poverty; or, if they were lucky, they received patronage from the wealthy, as Coleridge did through the generosity of Josiah Wedgwood II, manufacturer of Wedgwood bone china.

But for the academy, these artists and critics were degenerates, subversive of every right-thinking duty. As one Henri Rochefort wrote of Émile Zola in the Paris newspaper *L'Intransigeant* in 1903, "All the diseased minds, the topsy-turvy souls, the shady and the disabled, were ripe for the coming of the Messiah of Treason." So, artists made their own informal schools: Goethe's *Sturm und Drang*, Friedrich Schlegel's Romanticism, Impressionism's *Salon des Refusés*, Matisse's *Les Fauves* (wild beasts!), Expressionism's *Der Blaue Reiter*, Surrealism, Dada, the Beats, the Black Mountain poets, and beyond, as late as what the critic Robert Scholes called postmodern "fabulism" in the mid-twentieth century. In short, the arts have lived outside of the academy, *en plein air*, so to speak. Our problem is to understand how the arts might live again beyond the academy, beyond government subsidy, and beyond the media's middle-minded fixation on what merely conforms.

Literature. It's classic works and immortal figures. The Great Works preserved in a sacred tradition—you know, the Harvard Classics approach, designed to stand atop the family hearth. This much and no more. The canon. The civilizing of art and intellect's unruly natures.

Well, R.I.P. for all that.

Whether or not this death in the family is a good or bad thing, or a lot of both, is still open for debate. That debate is appropriate because the creation of a national literature, a Great Tradition, has, for lo these many years, been a struggle over who would have the social authority to determine what would and wouldn't count as literature. Hence, Dean Eliot's Harvard Classics. As the nation's premier scholarly institution, Harvard had the social authority to tell the rest of us what counted, what had "withstood the test of time." In the present, that sort of talk feels like a long con. What is worrying now is the uncertainty over what, if anything, will take that tradition's place, because it won't be professional literary critics, or programs like Mortimer Adler's "Great Books" curriculum at the University of Chicago, and it certainly won't be book reviewers in newspapers and magazines. Those reviewers and their journals have been eliminated by our preoccupation with social media, our life online, but that life has no interest in what is or isn't literary, is or isn't canonical.

As the late Morris Dickstein ("the last public intellectual") observed, the Internet offers global distribution but substitutes "the gripes and hosannas of ordinary readers for the authority of trained and experienced critics"—critics such as Lionel Trilling who in 1965 described the New York Intellectuals as a group that was "busy and vivacious about ideas, and, even more, about attitudes. Its assiduity constitutes an authority." Like Stefan Zweig, Dickstein was aware that he lived in a world that no longer existed, his own authority passing to people who were, in his view, unfit for the responsibility. Trilling was one of the first to see this coming in his essay "The Uncertain Future of the Humanistic Educational Ideal":

> At the present time in American society, there are few factors to be perceived, if any at all, which make it likely that within the next quarter-century there will be articulated in a convincing and effectual way an educational ideal that has a positive and significant connection with the humanistic educational traditions of the past.

The academy has offered little to no resistance to this trend in recent decades. Instead, it has focused on "identity politics." The consensus opinion has for some time been that any form of the traditional canon is in collaboration with a long history of discrimination, colonialism, and genocide. What's missing in this perspective is the certainty that the process of canon-making is not the same as the process of art-making. To say that canons are inherently bad things, or that there is no difference between canon-making and art-making is simply nihilistic. It's worth noting that right-wing nihilists have happily taken up what the left wing started, leading to the accelerating diminishment of the humanities in academia. If the professors don't think that the history of Western art is valuable, corporate governance sure as hell doesn't either.

Once upon a time, writers, publishers, and readers had more organic relationships, and that social organism had a more autonomous relationship to social authority. Art wasn't the plaything of the ruling class, or Harvard dons, nor did it languish under the censorious gaze of the awakened ones, and it wasn't an industry where vast sums of capital were at stake. The purpose of literary publishing was "publicizing" ideas that were both social and aesthetic. Publishing wasn't control over the shrinking circle of what could be thought; it was the subversion of that control.

When John Murray published the works of Lord Byron in London in the early nineteenth century, he risked prosecution and jail if the work was found to be blasphemous or libelous. Byron, notoriously, didn't help things, deliberately writing his poetry along the razor's edge of public tolerance, just as he lived his life. Percy Bysshe Shelley, for his part, wrote to his publisher, Thomas Hookham, regarding the appearance of his poem *Queen Mab*: "If you do not dread the arm of the law, or any exasperation of public opinion against yourself, I wish that it should be printed and published immediately." Hookham must have had such fears because he refused to publish the atheistic and revolutionary poem. Tory legislation against "blasphemous and seditious" literature was the order of the day.

As a consequence, the first edition of Shelley's poem was self-published in a run of a few hundred copies for distribution among friends. Even so, in 1817, the poem's radical politics and atheism were used against Shelley in his suit to gain the custody of his children; he lost the suit and never saw them afterward. Because of England's reactionary posture after the French Revolution and Napoleon's rise to power, poets and writers like Shelley, Byron, and Leigh Hunt found it safer to flee the country in order to write. They conducted their ongoing dialogue with their native land by way of brave, nerve-wracked, and sometimes imprisoned publishers.

At that time, there was little difference between a bookstore and a publisher: Bookstores produced the books they would sell. It was even possible to select your own cover board to match the binding of a new purchase to the other books in your library. It was a business completely engaged with a public. In fact, bookmaking and bookselling were then true "publicity," the rallying of public support for ideas, although personal fame, and often notoriety, became part of the equation, much to the author's surprise. As Byron commented after the success of his poem *Childe Harold's Pil-*

*grimage*, "I awoke one morning and found myself famous."

John Murray even hosted an afternoon tea for his writers, his "four o'clock friends." It may sound like a description of life on another planet, but a reader could go into Murray's store and buy a book, *Pride and Prejudice*, say, and hope to have tea with the author. (Emphasis on hope since Austen was a notorious homebody.)

"Biscuit, Miss Austen? Now tell me in all candor about this fellow Darcy . . ."

On the whole, writers did not take these risks in order to be regarded as geniuses, less still for inclusion in a canon monitored by experts. The poets and writers themselves were their own theorists and critics and their purpose was, foremost, life for themselves and, second, a plenitude of life for others, for the people of their world. This was a very new thing at the time. What Murray and friends created was autonomy and support for artists in the context of a like-minded community.

As late as the 1950s there remained some of this communitarian feel to bookstores, although the business of publishing had long ago been handed over to "professionals." For example, in my own San Francisco, there was Paul Elder's.

Paul Elder thought of himself as a "Western publisher" offering books like *Yosemite Legends* (1904) by Bertha Henry Smith, with illustrations by Florence Lundborg, a member of the arts group *Les Jeunes* ("the kids"), an association of bohemian writers and artists working in the tradition of European art dissidents. For seventy years, beginning in the 1890s, Paul Elder's was just a place to buy books. If you wanted a book, you told Paul about it. If you wanted to know about new books, he or his staff could tell you, or you could receive a print newsletter. Elder created a home for authors, books, and the people who read them.

The ideal of a publisher and bookstore in a community of readers is not entirely dead. City Lights Bookstore and Publisher has been around since 1953, and Deep Vellum Publisher and Bookstore in Dallas moves bravely forward, publishing not only its own list of innovative works but maintaining the backlist of Dalkey Archive Press, on which I have five books. But the point remains: Once the selection and manufacture of books became specialized, separating writers from publishers and retailers, and once the centralized manufacture of books required substantial capital, the chance that this new industry would offer resistance to free market capitalism was reduced to nothing. Publishers made profitable commodities and they kept the lid on ideas. It's hard to say which of those two purposes was the more important. As the novelist Ronald Sukenick once said to me, "What can you expect from Simon and Shoestore?" Or we might now ask, what can you expect from Amazon?

In 2010, I asked the late John O'Brien, legendary founder of Dalkey Archive, what he thought about the future of book publishing. He had this to say:

> The greatest threat to book publishing in the United States right now is Amazon. Through various spin-offs, they have become a publisher, and this means that they are moving towards becoming both a distributor of books and a publisher, and no book publisher will be able to compete.

Fifteen years later, Amazon's plan to control the production and distribution of book publishing is far from realized. But its assumptions about books and art culture in general are all too present. For Amazon, the printed book is just another "platform."

How is something called literature supposed to come out of this? If you thought it was hard to find a book spine-out at a Barnes and Noble superstore, try finding that book of poetry that changes your life, that you didn't even know you were looking for, on the web.

Now, through word of mouth or recommendations on websites like Goodreads, a few readers will find that book of poetry, although those will be, I suspect, mostly poets themselves, reduced now to a rarified species of hobbyist no greater in number than those enthusiasts who attend quilting fairs. But the population of readers interested in finding a transformative book will be ever smaller. Literature requires a culture, and not just a book culture, but a full culture, and the internet is not interested in creating cultures or autonomous communities. You will not have tea with

Jane Austen. You will not converse with the knowledgeable staff at Paul Elder's. Soon, you won't even get to sip coffee quietly at a Starbucks tucked into the rear of a Barnes and Noble superstore.

Taken together, this is murder for the future of books. But I wonder if there is much of a reason to grieve the passing of this Platonic Ideal we have called Literature, with its periods, its crafts, its canons of major and minor "figures," and, most precious, its faith that it is possible, as the critic W. K. Wimsatt once put it, for a work to "endure as a poetic monument." There are at present few things more Ozymandian than the idea of a poetic monument. The "great works," the classics, are themselves now "colossal wrecks," and their only context is a culture "boundless and bare." The respectful privilege we once reserved for a work like Shelley's "Ozymandias" now seems like something from a past full of childish illusions. You can no longer refer to a work as a "classic," as T. S. Eliot liked to say, without provoking a kind of amused condescension, as if to say, "You don't still believe in those, do you? It's so last century." The narrative of the "Great Works" has lost its legitimacy, and we have lost our credulity. If that past, the past of F. R. Leavis's "Great Tradition," is what literature seeks to preserve as its future, then I think it's easy to say that it has no future.

For those of us raised among the New Critics, it is downright Wagnerian to live in this twilight of the gods, and we will grieve their passing with whatever quiet dignity we can muster. But perhaps what we cared most about was never really "literature" anyway. Perhaps we've always suspected that, as William Carlos Williams wrote in *Kora in Hell*, "There is nothing sacred about literature, it is damned from one end to the other. There is nothing in literature but change and change is mockery."

Or, as Williams's friend Marianne Moore put it in her poem "Poetry": "I, too, dislike it" ... unless. Unless what we are talking about, unless what we are in danger of losing is of another order. There is still reason to mourn if what is passing out of our culture is what Wallace Stevens called poetry's "nobility." For Stevens, this nobility consisted in, at a minimum, two things that help us to live our still human lives. First, the Noble understands that literature's beauties are dependent upon, as Williams says, "change." Stevens put it this way in "Sunday Morning": "Death is the mother of beauty." It is the skillful openness to the world's transience that creates a clearing in which the beautiful can appear.

But for the Noble Rider, as Stevens called it in *The Necessary Angel*, there is something beyond beauty. What poetry provides, and what we are spiritually impoverished without, are those moments in which it reveals the Real, a reality fully aware of its own fictiveness, its own final place in the mind. It is not "Literature" that provides this understanding, it is the efficaciousness (the force, the power) of the poem, an efficaciousness that the poem itself expresses best. As Stevens wrote in "Not Ideas About the Thing but the Thing Itself," contemplating the cry of a bird:

> That scrawny cry—it was
>
> A chorister whose c preceded the choir.
>
> It was part of the colossal sun,
>
> Surrounded by its choral rings,
>
> Still far away. It was like
>
> A new knowledge of reality.

This human Good cannot be touched by the dissolution of the institution of literature, let alone by what happens to our dismal book industry. The sordid avarice of media empires and their pimping of "content" cannot harm this Good, this Nobility. Literature may not have a future, but it will have its own peculiar eternity.

Given how far modern literary publishing has come from its origins, from publisher-bookstores like John Murray's and Paul Elder's, and how concentrated it is now in corporate monopolies, it's a little late to get weepy over its demise. My feeling is: Let it go. It has always been compromised.

The institutions of literature have always worked against the life of the work of art as much as they have worked for it.

Historically, literary institutions have done two things well. First, they have managed the unruliness of language by creating canons of the major, the minor, and the non-canonical or irrelevant. If the purpose of a poem or novel is, in Viktor Shklovsky's term, to "enstrange" the world as we know it and open it up to the possibility of alternate arrangements, canonization can only serve the opposite purpose: to stabilize, to habituate. In other words, in literary or art canons the work becomes part of an ideological apparatus, whether religious, aristocratic, capitalist, socialist, or ballyhooed multicultural.

Herbert Marcuse put it this way in *One-Dimensional Man*:

> What they [the Romantics] recall and preserve in memory pertains to the future: images of a gratification that would dissolve the society which suppresses it. What has been invalidated is [literature's] subversive force, [its] destructive content—[its] truth . . . The absorbent power of society depletes the artistic dimension by assimilating its antagonistic contents.

Canons do indeed tend to invalidate art's subversive force, but this fact should not be understood as a renunciation of the works in themselves. Taken on their own terms, nearly all of the individual works within the established art canons—whether literature, music, or painting—were in their time formally subversive, to use Marcuse's word, in one way or another, and beautifully so. The artist's purpose has always been to "make it new," in Ezra Pound's enduring phrase, and to hell with those who want art to merely echo the past.

This brings me to the second thing that canons do well: They celebrate their victims. True, many artists do yearn for the sort of enduring fame that canonization claims to offer. But the power of their work, when it is authentic, is its indifference to what the critics and makers of canons think. Of the English Romantics, Keats was the most keenly aware of this difficulty. In a letter to painter Benjamin Haydon, Keats wrote, "There is no greater Sin after the 7 deadly than to flatter oneself into an idea of being a great Poet."

As for the promise of digital culture and our Amazonian future: Can it produce a literature that works through the spirit of change, of enstrangement, of refusal, and in which a sense of beauty overcomes all other considerations? Perhaps. But it's helpful to remember what a rich and difficult thing Keatsian beauty is. His poetry enstranges by re-collecting an object's original intimacy. The poem breaks the crust of habitual expectation and stereotype by abandoning the self's ordinary perspective in an act of sympathy for the existential integrity of others, even if only for a sparrow. In a letter to his friend Benjamin Bailey, Keats wrote:

> I scarcely remember counting upon any Happiness—I look not for it if it be not in the present hour—nothing startles me beyond the Moment. The setting sun will always set me to rights—or if a Sparrow come before my Window I take part in its existence and pick about the Gravel.

This is "negative capability," the ability to join in the being of something other than yourself.

Can this deference to the dignity of being happen in the context of an internet dominated by corporations whose job is to create rigid market identities so it can better sell them? For a modern writer—whether conventionally published or self-published on Amazon—commercial liftoff happens when brand recognition is achieved. Is it possible to do your business on the internet and be alienated, which is to say outside of it? You won't easily find the particularity of Keats's sparrow there, or Marianne Moore's toads, or Williams's wheelbarrow, or Pound's "petals on a wet, black bough."

Worse yet, many writers today seem willing to play the game, creating fan pages and personal web sites promoting their brand. The writing community, such as it is, seems almost sick with desire for this ephemeral grace. In the World According to Google, it is not possible to be alienated because there is nothing outside of it! The internet is, in the worst possible sense, as Hegel wrote, "the night in which all cows are black." The merit of any given book is now restricted to the spectacle of money congratulating itself.

As Andrei Codrescu wrote in his prescient book *The Disappearance of the Outside* (1990):

> The notion of community has been stripped of its direction. No longer does community—any community—stand outside the State, in direct challenge to it. All communities have been reoriented through a neat trick of generalization to become the State, an electronic Superstate that is a combination of traditional nationalism and electronic globalism. When community was a means of resistance, it was constituted to point from the inside out: it proceeded from a center of internal concerns to make progressively wider contacts with the outside world. The community redesigned by the State points inward: it is a producer of silence.

In the era of Siri and the AI Chatbot, we might now add, yes, but it is a voluble silence. It never shuts up.

And as Marshall McLuhan observed in his famous *Playboy* interview:

> As a man molded within the literate Western tradition, I do not personally cheer the dissolution of that tradition through the electric involvement of all the senses: I don't enjoy the destruction of neighborhoods by

> high-rises or revel in the pain of identity quest. No one could be less enthusiastic about these radical changes than myself.

McLuhan's challenge is to discover how to relate to these technologies without being mere unconscious "servomechanisms," as he called those who uncritically embrace inhumanly powerful gadgets. Addressing that problem begins with an honest evaluation of what these mechanisms are, who we are, and what it is that we want. What art wants, as Marcuse articulated it sixty years ago, is "images of a gratification that would dissolve the society which suppresses it." Unfortunately, in the world of the happy servomechanism it is artists and their communities that are dissolved, digested, and totalized.

Wallace Stevens once wrote that poetry is a "destructive force," and that it can "kill a man." In the modernist era of the great art-isms, whether Surrealism, Imagism, or fascist Futurism, this was a plausible claim. In the present, however, all such pronouncements are laughable because they are spoken into a technological echo chamber. How happy we are when we post something and twenty-five people press a button claiming to "like" it. The version of this essay originally published at *Lapham's Quarterly*'s website had 527 likes and a bonus 206 tweets. It's enough to make you want to do it again! But, in the end, all we hear is the reassuring sound of our own voices becoming more bug-like with every passing year, full of the digital clicking emitted by Kafka's wounded beetle, an apple embedded in his side.

The fact to be overcome is this: Our rulers need spend very little time worrying about what artists are up to. They don't need strategies for managing their disruptions. Literature on the internet comes with its own self-management. And this for a simple reason: It cannot sufficiently distinguish itself from the vast reaches of mere "content." But I remain Nietzschean enough not to want to give aid and comfort to my jailer by calling a prison house a pleasure dome.

## THE GREAT REFUSAL: HUNGRY FREAKS, DADDY

> My circus animals were all on show,
> Those stilted boys, that burnished chariot,
> Lion and woman and the Lord knows what.
>
> **—W. B. Yeats, "The Circus Animals' Desertion"**

I cannot and should not tell you, reader, what your "resistance" should look like. Unlike Timothy Snyder, I don't have twenty recommendations for resisting tyranny, the money-eyed world. My only advice for busting out of the money prison is simply to move on to the next joyful deed in the company of others, in association with friends, conceptual co-conspirators, and actual comrades in the garden, on the project, in the chapel, on the meditation cushion, and in the streets, when necessary, with music, poetry, and art providing assurances that we are going about this struggle in the right way.

My story will take a personal turn now because, as Henry David Thoreau wrote in Walden, "I should not talk about myself if there were anyone whom I knew as well."

I was born in San Lorenzo, California, a post-war tract home development, a "vet-village," in the San Francisco East Bay. It was a colorless environment to grow up in. But in the late 1960s, it felt to me as if life was at last beginning to happen, and not far away, just down the block. In particular, the six blocks of Telegraph Avenue leading to U. C. Berkeley and Sproul Plaza, site of Mario Savio's Free Speech protest, was a place of awakening for me. My high school pals and I would pile in a '52 Chevrolet and drive up the Nimitz and then the stately Warren freeways, the Doors's "Light My Fire" as loud as possible on the radio (long version, of course, played on KSAN—hippy radio).

We'd get off at the Berkeley exit, drive past the bone-white otherworldliness of the old Claremont Hotel, and suddenly arrive in the Land of Otherwise: Berkeley. The colors seemed more intense there, mostly the iridescent green aura of trees: coast redwood, ponderosa pine, and blue gum eucalyptus. My spiritual antennae seemed to say, "Okay, pay attention. You might actually be alive now."

Comically, we ourselves were not much like the place. We wore our suburban uniforms of the day: short-sleeve madras shirts, wool sweater-vests, Levi's, and brown suede saddle shoes. We called this look "college" (pronounced co-*leege*), although I doubt that we could have said why. Into Vaughn at Sather Gate we'd go, that venerable (and now long defunct) clothier of frat boys. (It was the sort of place that you could imagine Dobie Gillis buying his shirts, if you remember him. Sigh. Maynard G. Krebs?) The freaks on Telegraph Avenue would laugh as we walked by, lined up like goslings lacking a mother. But their laughter was gentle and indulgent. I understood what they meant. I laughed at us, too.

But after Vaughn, we had more serious purposes: Odyssey Records (in a storefront later to be the home of Rasputin's Records). That was our real destination. I bought John Mayall's *A Hard Road*, with the heart-stopping guitar of Peter Green; Blue Cheer's over-the-top *Vincebus Eruptum* (controlled chaos) with its primordial cover of Eddie Cochran's great refusal of work, "Summertime Blues"; Paul Butterfield's *East/West* with Michael Bloomfield and Elvin Bishop's blues raga; as well as records by Bay Area bands like Big Brother and the Holding Company, Country Joe and the Fish, and, of course, the Dead. I'd play those records at night on my Sears portable record player and listen within the interstellar remove that headphones provide. This was where I wanted to live, with bass notes blossoming in my skull, that sympathetic bone.

All of this led me, a working-class suburban boy, into a state of permanent dismay with the world that I had been first thrown into. I was and am utterly loyal to the first feeling of pleasure, play, open possibility, and freedom that I experienced in the dear '60s, a time when everything and anything seemed possible even in a social and political context that was murderous. But that was the world of straight cats, and we were heading toward something different. It felt like I was being saved, or experiencing grace.

Even as an undergraduate at the University of San Francisco, when I decided to major in English, I knew that what I was doing would not likely allow me to live a recognizable American life, certainly not like the lives I knew from my suburban origins. In most ways, I thought that was a good thing. If being realistic and secure meant living in the way I'd grown up, I was happy to make myself insecure. It wasn't that I risked joblessness when I became a student of literature; I sought joblessness just to make sure that the bridge back to suburbia was thoroughly burned. Nonetheless, the idea that I would not be able to sustain indefinitely this life among books was clear to me. But I got used to being poor, and so I thought, "If poverty is all I have to fear, I'm ready for that. I'll do this until something or someone tells me I have to stop."

I felt like Thomas Merton, the Christian contemplative and Trappist monk, who believed that going to university and studying literature was his first step out of the worldly empire of money and into the monastery. In his autobiographical work, *The Seven Storey Mountain*, Merton wrote:

> This registration in the graduate school represented the first remote step of a retreat from the fight for money and fame, from the active and worldly life of conflict and competition. If anything, I would now be a teacher, and live the rest of my life in the relative peace of a college campus, reading and writing books.

As in the Parable of the Burning House in *The Lotus Sutra*, Merton had to "walk through the door" or die in flames.

That's how I felt, too.

Just as this aesthetic and spiritual education was taking form, I made a similarly fruitful political discovery. In the summer of 1969, I joined a group of Marxist autodidacts in a rented office space in downtown Hayward and, using materials from the American Friends Service Committee, prepared to be a draft counselor. In that office were magazines—*Ramparts, The Berkeley Barb, The San Francisco Oracle*—and pamphlets analyzing our motives for being in the war—the role of money and militarism—and revealing the true facts of what our "boots on the ground" meant to the people of Vietnam and to our own soldiers. I remember how surprised I was by all this. I'd never seen anything like it. It certainly wasn't the sort of stuff I was offered in high school. But I reached a quick conclusion: "Oh," I thought, "this is what it's like to think. This is what honesty feels like. Somebody is bothering to tell me the truth. This is what I can be loyal to." I'd never felt so alive before. Not one of the dead, not another creature of my culture, not another cog in the wheel—alive.

I would go on to more sophisticated versions of this experience as a university student, reading the usual suspects, the intellectual heroes of the era, Herbert Marcuse, Theodore Roszak, and eventually Marx and the pantheon of Western Marxist intellectuals, especially Theodor Adorno and Antonio Negri. But I had learned something in that grim little office in Hayward that I couldn't learn elsewhere, not even from Adorno. I learned that this critical intelligence, this truth-telling, this honesty, does not happen in the big world, it happens in dingy little spaces set apart and inhabited by "freaks," a demographic that seemed happily inexhaustible in the Bay Area at the time. In other words, my political and personal anagnorisis came among people who had dropped out of the world as we'd known it. It came within a counterculture, a second step out of the worldly empire of money.

Contrary to the common assumption that the 1960s counterculture was all about hippies, communal living, and the art and music of psychedelia, it was in truth a vortex of energies. Allen Ginsberg was mistaken to limit the counterculture's "tribes" to freaks and leftists. There were in fact many tribes all in the orbit of an historic Great Refusal. These tribes attempted to create a revolution in everyday life, the utopian project that anarchist Bernard Marszalek, in his book *Jobs, Jive, and Joy*, calls "radical hedonism."

First and foremost, the counterculture was about taking refuge in what Ingmar Bergman called the "little world," because, the broader world "is a den of thieves and night is falling . . . Let us be kind, generous, affectionate and good." (*Fanny and Alexander*) The spirit informing this "little world" was play, and, for the large part, the form that play took was art. Like the Beat hipster of the 1950s, freak culture was deeply attuned to the arts through psychedelic poster art (surrealism for the people), novels and poetry like Richard Brautigan's *Trout Fishing in America* and Sylvia Plath's *The Bell Jar*, and that noodling discourse that was a Jerry Garcia guitar solo.

Then there was the New Left which began as a reaction to the War in Vietnam and continued as a Marxist adventure that was humanistic rather than Leninist, with a focus on the problem of human "alienation," inspired by Marx's early writings like *Economic and Philosophic Manuscripts of 1844*. The Frankfurt School Marxist Herbert Marcuse was the "father of the New Left."

The era also welcomed Black Power and the Black Panthers across the Bay in Oakland. As Marcuse said in a 1971 speech at UC Berkeley, "I still consider the radical student movement and the Black and Brown militants as the only real opposition we have in this country." But counterculture was part of this mix, too. The Panthers learned something that projects like the Haight Street Diggers figured out first: taking refuge in the local, especially food banks and medical clinics, in something like what we now call "mutual support" networks.

Then there was Second Wave feminism which in its early years was in cahoots with the counterculture. Bra burning was a gesture not only of defiance but of solidarity with the burning of draft cards. Sisters were commonly found in playful paisley bellbottoms, braless and bare-armed, laughing and looking. Germaine Greer's 1970 polemic *The Female Eunuch* is irreverent, funny, in keeping with the creative dissent of the period, and supportive of women's rediscovery of . . . lust? She later wrote that her book was about "the freedom to run, shout, talk loudly, and sit with your knees apart."

Even Gloria Steinem was, to a degree, a feminist flower child and an advocate for sexual liberation: denim and tinted glasses, miniskirts, she was sex-positive before the fact. Posing as a Playboy bunny was not entirely foreign to Steinem's nature; she too was a freedom-loving pleasure seeker. Her first work, *The Beach Book*, explained that the "beach is not a place but a state of mind," and that there are important "things to do by yourself when no one is watching." She later had her own version of Ginsberg's "gathering of the tribes" in bringing feminism and Black Power together in the essay "After Black Power, Women's Liberation."

And, of course, there was the environmental movement which was beginning to recognize itself as a movement through Stewart Brand's *Whole Earth Catalog* in 1968. Brand was most interested in grassroots activism through DIY living; his motto was "access to tools." His catalog was essential to the counterculture's "back to the land" labors.

Usually overlooked in summaries of the counterculture is an important fact—important because it is the only thing that has survived more or less intact—that the era welcomed the arrival of Eastern religions and their contrary way of looking at the world. Buddhism proceeds "against the stream of the world." This path had been prepared by the beatnik culture of the 1950s, but the real turning point was the visit by the Beatles to India in 1968 to study Transcendental Meditation with the Maharishi Mahesh Yogi. Lewis Lapham covered the occasion for the *Saturday Evening Post* and concluded his book *With the Beatles* (2005) with this vision:

> The weather that morning was as strange as the light in an El Greco painting, and on the farther shore, clearly visible in the forest of teak and seshum trees, two figures were standing in bright sunlight, holding flowers in their hands, listening to the voice of the cosmos.

Meanwhile, the gay rights movement was gathering its energies beginning with the Stonewall Riot in Greenwich Village in 1969. In the same year, the Gay Liberation Front was organized in reaction to Stonewall, modeling itself after the New Left. And then in 1970 the first Gay Pride Parades were launched in San Francisco, Los Angeles, and Chicago. I once watched the parade move up Market Street toward the Civic Center, joyful and defiant as any freak fest or anti-war demonstration.

Finally, there were AIM, the American Indian Movement, and IAT, Indians of All Tribes. AIM raised awareness of systemic poverty, discrimination, and police brutality, while IAT's occupation of the former federal prison on Alcatraz Island in 1969 made hopeful noise in an already radicalized Bay Area. In more recent years, Native American tribes have joined forces with environmental groups to protest the continued destruction of Mother Earth.

What happened to the counterculture's "coat of many colors"? Where is it now? Vanished in what Gore Vidal called, "The United States of Amnesia."

Taken together, the varied refuseniks that made up the Great Refusal were rebels for a cause: to create an alternative reality, to reject alienation and repression, and to play in the *jouissance* of life, unfettered by what was merely habitual in a dying world. It was the continuation of the old effort to unite socialism and anarchy, Marx and Bakunin, revolution and play. Unlike the progressive politics of the present, the many parties to the counterculture had no sense of fixed "identity." The Great Refusal was fluid, interpenetrating, and, consequently, it felt like freedom. We learned from each other.

Beginning in the late 1970s, this vortex of energies began to wobble and spin like a dying star throwing off the last of its bright force. Counterculture's varied purposes began to recalibrate within universities, leaving whatever remained of communalism out in the woods to "do its own thing" where no one could see it. Feminism, the New Left, and even Black Power were seeking tenure under the mantle of a united discipline, Cultural Studies. That seemed natural enough at first, given the student radicalism of the time. We didn't worry about it because we had come to trust each other. Universities felt like places of refuge and resistance.

But in the end, it was a catastrophe for resistance. First, the emphasis on class soon fell away, displaced by American-style Cultural Studies and its obsession with popular culture seen through a feminist or racial lens. As British Marxist Stuart Hall commented at the time, "I don't know what to say about American Cultural Studies. I am completely dumbfounded by it." Second, the idea that art could be a "site of resistance" fell victim to the counter-idea that art and artists couldn't be trusted to keep to the program created by the progressive illuminati. After thirty years of identity politics and censorship by campus culture cops of what was not sufficiently "correct," what was too white and too male, or, conversely, what was too weird or risky, artists began to fear not only evangelical nationalism and militarism but themselves. We lost trust in ourselves. We could get canceled!

After the canon wars of the 1980s and '90s shamed the art of the past, and after decades of self-censorship by writers and artists, the humanities and arts stand naked, friendless—easy pickings for war on the Woke, a painful example of political self-immolation. As Julie Caniglia wrote as early as 1996, in the Minneapolis *City Pages*:

> The multiculturalism that appeared so revolutionary ten years ago has curdled into a fractious politics of identity, resulting in a new and, for the most part, banal didacticism . . . As art gets parsed into a multitude of niches based on identity, it follows that the standards for judging such work are lowered, eliminated, or qualified into irrelevance.

## THE FICTION CORRECTIVE

> "How should literature respond to a reality that is equal parts vapid and violent, where the celebration of mediocrity is correlated with an utter disregard for human life."—**Jess Bergman, *The Nation,* January 2026**

In 1979, my first book of fiction, *Heretical Songs,* was accepted by the Fiction Collective, and the trajectory of my life began to take form. Working with the other writers in the Collective began almost immediately; we were a collective, after all, and I was expected to help out. I can't tell you how right being published by a "collective" felt. It would have suited me fine if they'd called it the Fiction Commune. I thought, "That's where I belong, among friends, artists, and comrades, and not in the indecipherable world of New York publishing."

Raymond Federman, Fanny Howe, Ronald Sukenick, and Jonathan Baumbach had been running the place out of Brooklyn College and overseeing the day-to-day activities of the press. I'm not sure just how front and center the press was for them. For sure, none of them felt born to book publishing, and not unreasonably, because they were writers, good writers, and they would have preferred to be left alone to do their work. Baumbach thought of the situation as an emergency that would end soon. After all, they were mostly New York writers and publishing through the established houses was their birthright. "I couldn't imagine us going on indefinitely," Baumbach wrote, "When would we find the time to write our books?"

In short, the thing that got the Collective started was not any zeal for publishing as such but a commitment to American literature's need for an eclectic and generally outré sense of beauty. Ron, Jon, Fanny, and Ray were perfectly serious about that.

And then there was the unavoidable fact of New York's deracinated, fleshless book industry. It was turning heavily against all things "experimental," anything smelling of the 1960s, especially the laughter . . . the laughter . . . of the '60s, the Dionysian plenty that John Hawkes captured so perfectly in his novel *The Blood Oranges*. Or Kurt Vonnegut's dark laughter in *Slaughterhouse-Five*, Joseph Heller's ditto in *Catch 22*, Joan Didion's calculated charm in *White Album*, Donald Barthelme's surreal laughter in *The Dead Father*, Robert Coover's inside jokes in *The Universal Baseball Association*, Richard Brautigan's happy hippy smirk in *Trout Fishing in America*, Stanley Elkin's shtick in *The Living End*, and Ishmael Reed's neo-hoodoo hijinks in *Yellow Back Radio Broke-Down*.

And yet no previous American writers had been more intent on the seriousness of the joke—the blackness of the merriment, as in Stanley Kubrick and Terry Southern's hooting vision of apocalypse in *Dr. Strangelove*—at least not since Nathanael West's *The Day of the Locust*, or Mark Twain's *Letters from the Earth*. For this reason, the first moniker that stuck with the writers of the 1960s and '70s was not "postmodernist" but "black humorist." Lamentably, in the present, it is as David Samuels wrote in an essay in *County Highway*: "Laughter is a danger to the corporate monopoly pipelines and content-aggregation businesses. It could make someone mad and ruin your brand."

A few years earlier, Fanny and Jon had experienced notable successes with commercial publishers (Fanny with Houghton Mifflin, Jon with Random House), but they saw as early as 1973 what direction publishing would take once corporate conglomeration set in. For instance, Ron's first two books of fiction were published by the Dial Press, an independent house since 1923, editor-in-chief E. L. Doctorow. It had been owned since 1967 by Dell Publishing, which was purchased by Doubleday in 1976. Doubleday dissolved Dial Press in 1985, but it was revived and became part of Bantam/Doubleday/Dell, then Random House, then Penguin Random House, and finally it went into *die pfoten* of the German media giant Bertelsmann—once the central publishing organ of the Nazi Party, employing Jewish slave labor in its printing houses in Lithuania.

Prior to these profit-minded consolidations, Dial was the publisher of controversial works like Norman Mailer's *An American Dream*, James Baldwin's *The Fire Next Time*, and H. Rap Brown's *Die Nigger Die!* But then the Big Chill set in. Most notoriously, Jerry Rubin left the Yippies for Wall Street, the very place where he had satirically dropped real dollar bills in 1967. The '60s may have been dead, but the Fiction Collective said, "Long live what is lively!" In short, the Fiction Collective was created because New York publishing houses were in the process of being entombed within corporate media empires, within which they are sunk to this day, ever more deeply.

By the late 1970s, anything that lacked the bona fides of realism was officially suspect. The battle cry of that moment was "Real People!" The realist aesthetic that the book industry adopted is the brine most apprentice writers have pickled in for the last half century. The requirement of realist procedures now "goes without saying," as any literary agent will explain, although she will usually explain it in terms of "sincerity." You know, sincerity, not irony. It is not only the dominant aesthetic but the dominant ideology for anyone hoping to publish with one of New York's commercial publishers. The artful realism of Henry James, Theodore Dreiser, Edith Wharton, and John Steinbeck has been turned into an ideology. Realism is now what the Marxist critic Stuart Hall called an ideological "of course." It is the form in which the corporate political economy, and even a complicit progressive left, tells its stories. But it wasn't Ernest Hemingway's American realism that had thus won. It was capitalist realism.

Of course, in these early days of the AI reordering of all things human, this battle within the larger culture wars has been made to seem insignificant. Whether realist or antirealist, we are up against the same problem: the end of reading, the end of the book, and certainly the end of anything as quaint as aesthetics. AI gives not a fuck about beauty.

## A TIDE OF SHIT

> I'm filled with the sadness that afflicted the Roman patricians of the fourth century: I feel irredeemable barbarism rising from the bowels of the earth . . . I have always tried to live in an ivory tower, but a tide of shit is beating at its walls, threatening to undermine it.
>
> —**Gustave Flaubert in a letter to Ivan Turgenev**

In 1989 the Fiction Collective became Fiction Collective Two or FC2. Ron Sukenick and I ran the shop with the aid of our respective universities, the University of Colorado and Illinois State University. Six years later, Boulder's support was withdrawn and by 1999 I was ready to hand the Collective off to Ralph Berry at Florida State University in Tallahassee. But Ron and I had one last monumental hurrah!, relevant to my theme and worthy of your attention. Let me tell you that story. It is not only a better story but a story that we lived. Oh, how we lived it. We lived it and then some.

Our last hurrah started with a phone call from Jim Sitter. At the time, he was directing CLMP (Council for Literary Magazines and Presses), a service organization for not-for-profit publishers like FC2. But Jim's real stature at that moment came from the fact that he had single-handedly done what no one thought possible. He had gained the ear of major national foundations, most notably the Lila Wallace-Reader's Digest Fund (from the *Readers Digest* fortune, ironically) and the Mellon Foundation.

Sitter himself was a piece of work. He looked like Tim Robbins in Robert Altman's *The Player*. He kept an immaculately trimmed beard and wore stylish but outdoorsy clothes: lots of wool and leather and always topped with a fedora. He had a look. The Sitter look. A synthesis of Hollywood and the Vermont Country Store. He also had a style. I have never known a person more measured in what he allowed himself to say. His very presence said, "I know something. Actually, I know a lot of things. These are things you'd like to know, but I'm not going to tell you, mostly because I don't trust you not to use what I know to fuck things up."

Jim's style also said, "You can ask questions and I will carefully answer them, but you will never know all that you want to know. You will only know what I need you to know." Jim was my introduction to the atmosphere that surrounds philanthropy, its secret wisdom. A sort of "we know you better than you know yourself; we even know what you need better than you do." This was all condescending and insufferable, especially for book people.

So, Jim had carefully put together this fragile alliance between CLMP, the NEA, and Big Philanthropy, all for the benefit of literary publishers, but I think he lived in the fear that we writers and publishers would mess it all up. Which of course we did. And now here comes FC2 and its edgy books: Samuel R. Delany's *Hogg*, Cris Mazza's *Is it Sexual Harassment Yet?*, Jeffrey DeShell's *S&M*, Doug Rice's *Blood of Mugwump*, and many others.

And then on one warm Illinois spring day in 1995, I got a call from Jim.

"How many of your books give credit for support to the NEA?"

See? No prologue, no context, no effort to allow me to understand why my answers were important before I answered. I don't even think he took the time to say, "Hi," he just asked the question he needed an answer to.

"All of them except one," I replied.

"Just the ones you listed in your grant application to the NEA?"

"No, all of them. I thought that the NEA would like it if . . ."

I could feel tension and maybe a groan on the other side.

He interrupted impatiently, "That was a mistake."

"Why?"

"You shouldn't have done that."

"If the NEA has a problem, why haven't I heard from Cliff?"

Cliff Becker was the director of the literature section of

the NEA. He was a prince in every possible way. He was the anti-Sitter. Completely open but also smart and sympathetic. He really liked what the small presses were about, even FC2. Sadly, he died of a heart attack in 2005 at the age of forty.

Sitter replied, "Cliff can't talk to you now. He can't be seen as coaching your replies."

"Our replies to what?"

At last he came to it. "Jesse Helms in the Senate and Pete Hoekstra in the House are using your books to demand the end of the NEA, or the end of funding literature, or a reduction in the NEA's budget, which it seems very likely they will get. This is really going to put [President Clinton's NEA chair] Jane [Alexander] on the spot."

"Oh."

"It's just politics, it's just a way for them to play to conservatives, to have something for their fundraising, but it's also very dangerous."

We were a potential liability for the NEA, and, of course, we were also a threat to the little empire Jim was creating. He was trying to make literature a philanthropic field, something corporations could give money to comfortably, like opera. Naturally, he hoped to make himself indispensable to that future. And we were messing that up.

I said, "Oh," again.

"If you are contacted by the press or by staffers to Helms or anyone else, don't say anything."

"Can't we defend our . . ."

He nearly screamed, "Curt, these are not nice people. They don't care who gets hurt. You need to be careful. I'll let you know if we need a statement from you." Which was his way of saying that if he needed a statement from us, he'd write it.

Saying nothing was not in my nature, but I tried to be a team player.

"Okay," I said.

"I'll get back to you if anything comes up."

"All right. Thanks, Jim."

Later that day or the next I was contacted by a reporter from *The Washington Times*, the Moonie paper-of-record for all things contemptible. The reporter, a woman with a very pleasant voice, asked for a comment and I thought, "She will twist anything I say to her own purposes, plus Jim told me to shut up," so I said, "No comment." Of course, she twisted my silence to her own purpose. She made me look bad, like I was hiding something, which I was. I was hiding the fact that the NEA didn't trust me to talk.

I was also contacted by Christian conservative Allen Wildmon of the American Family Association. That was a surreal experience. Wildmon went on in his homespun, vicious way trying to get a comment out of me, something he could put in a fundraising brochure, something to label me un-American, and, honestly, just about anything I said could have suited that purpose pretty well. I am un-American in a fundamentally patriotic way, understanding, along with Samuel Johnson, that "patriotism is the last refuge of the scoundrel."

Anyway, it was revelatory to be in a position where I could hear the snake in Wildmon's voice, and in the voice's contours, and let it just fill me and allow me to know it. Thrilling, but a little scary. He came on all cornpone, and, "Heck, what do you think about all this?" Meanwhile, he's holding a noose behind his back.

Afterwards, it occurred to me, "Wildmon. It was he and his brother Donald that went after Robert Mapplethorpe. Hey, we're the new Mapplethorpe!"

I felt something like pride rinse over me.

What had happened was this. In performing its ordinary if malignant due diligence, hoping to turn up some smut to hurl at the NEA, a staffer for Representative Pete Hoekstra had come across one of our books. I actually had a telephone conversation with the staffer. He called, identified himself as part of Hoekstra's office, and asked me to send him copies of all of our books giving credit to the NEA.

I asked him how they had found out about us.

"I was sitting in a coffee shop, and I read a review of one of your books in *The Washington Post*."

"Well, that was easy," I thought.

During that time, in large part because of our Black Ice

Books, there was no shortage of sexually edgy material just waiting for the wrong Southern Baptist to discover.

He continued. "I went to a bookstore, looked at the copyright page for the NEA logo, read a bit of it, and brought it back to the office."

He was very matter-of-fact. Not scandalized, not apologetic, and not cynical. The painful part for me was that getting a prominent review in the *Post* was usually a cause for celebration, but now it appeared that even our successes would be used against us. I supposed that if we were going to keep NEA support, we would just have to stop being noticed.

The review was of our first Chick-Lit anthology, *Chick-Lit: Postfeminist Fiction*, edited by Cris Mazza and Jeffrey DeShell. The reviewer was a novelist, Carolyn See, and it was not positive. In fact, as I noted on first reading, it was irresponsible. After complaining about the lack of plot in the stories, she wrote, "You never saw so many wigs and crew cuts bleached white, or so many female genitalia . . . Not many straight women here either . . . The National Endowment for the Arts funded part of this enterprise, and it is couched in words and concepts that are sure to give Jesse Helms a conniption fit."

This open appeal to Helms in a Washington newspaper, for God's sake, may be the worst thing I have ever known a writer to do to fellow writers. The incredible irony is that in the 1950s Ms. See made a living testifying for the defense in pornography trials of books like *Lust Thy Friends and Neighbors*. Even crazier, her own father wrote seventy-three hardcore pornography novels, as she attests in *Blue Money*, her memoir of the period.

But she was shocked, just shocked, at *Chick-Lit*.

> You smile with pomp & rigor: you talk of benevolence & virtue;
>
> I act with benevolence & Virtue & get murder'd time after time. —William Blake, *Jerusalem*

And then on September 17, 1995, Jesse Helms took to the Senate floor waving Doug Rice's *Blood of Mugwump*—an omni-gendered outrage fit to make William Burroughs blush—over his head and complaining about how it had traumatized the impressionable young people on his staff. He was arguing for a bill sponsored by John Ashcroft to defund the NEA. Waving the book as if it were McCarthy's list of commies in the State Department, he said, "This book called *Blood of Mug . . . Mugwump* . . . I've never heard of the author . . . is repugnant to the values . . ." and so on.

Jesse Helms's death in 2008 was the closest he ever came to honesty. There's an inevitable frankness about dying. The ugly truth takes off its mask. Even so, he probably raised a desperate "question of personal privilege" about it, thus putting himself in the merciful hands of the great parliamentarian in the sky, who ruled against him, obviously. A perplexed Helms discovered himself to be, at last, just another ghost, immortally "roamin' in the gloamin'" of this Bardo we call Life on Earth.

I'd have thought it was all good fun if Sitter and the NEA hadn't been freaking out. They made no effort to defend us or our books. They set us adrift.

It would have been nice to live in a world where Jane Alexander could sit before Congress and say, "Senator Helms, do you Republicans read? Like, at all? Have you read, for example, Greek mythology? Are you familiar with the story of Procne and Philomela? After Procne's husband Tereus rapes her sister Philomela and cuts out her tongue so she can't accuse him, Procne chops Tereus's children up, cooks them in a stew, and feeds them to him. Well, *Mugwump* retells that story, among others. Is that still 'repugnant to your values'? Then, Western civilization is repugnant to your values. And that, frankly, is as it should be, given what you are."

But, as you know, we don't live in that world. Jane Alexander is a Hollywood actress whom Clinton named NEA chair because he thought she'd be too pretty for all those Republican pricks to be mean to, but I guess southern gallantry really is dead.

In the end, the situation was this: The NEA can fund art if it doesn't fund art. Or it can fund art so long as nobody finds out about it. Jane Alexander would have been better off if she'd told Cliff to give us the money in hundred-dollar bills stuffed in a plain manila envelope. I'll tell you this, although we played along with the team, shut up and let them handle it, we did not get an NEA grant the next year. FC2 did not receive an NEA in the following thirty years. We could have listed *Hamlet* on our application and they would have refused it.

So, let me say now what I would like to have said then. In the end, the NEA is a bureaucracy assigned the task of managing art, not aiding it. Or put it this way: It does not provide support to art that offends its masters. Indifferent to what offends the bosses, publishers like FC2 go about their business of re-energizing the idea that narrative art can still matter as social and, in its own way, spiritual antagonist.

Spiritual antagonist? Yes. Because when narrative art is not merely a confirmation of dominant ideology, when it is not just another domestic drama that does nothing more than confirm the world we already know, the work of art is an act of refusal. A refusal to live in a dead world, the boss's world, money's world. Art is the one place where life insists on living. And that is spiritual.

Oh, and Hoekstra's staffer? When he asked me to send him all of our books, I said, "Go buy your own copies. We could use the sales."

The pathetic coda to all of this took place a month or so after the Helms tirade. My local congressman, Thomas Ewing, acknowledged as the stupidest man in Congress by his peers, informed the press that he would be making a personal visit to my university president to discuss the NEA controversy and my role in it. I didn't think I could be fired on the request of a congressman, and the administration had a strong record of defending the arts against censorship, so I wasn't worried. Much. Ewing was informed that it was a university matter and no concern of his. (Man, has that idea gone away.) Then, they talked about the weather, corn, and the men's basketball team for fifteen minutes, just to give the impression of a "frank exchange of ideas."

Yes, I had caused some trouble that I'm sure the administration could have done without, but what did they expect? If you let working-class artist-radicals into the ivory tower, there's gonna be some gobsmacking. I was a professor, one of the privileged, but I did not know the "rules of the game" and I had no intention of learning them.

# TAKE BACK YOUR EMPTINESS

Beyond a certain point there's no return. That's the point that must be reached.

—Franz Kafka, *The Zürau Aphorisms*

## MAKE YOURSELF USELESS

> A poet only to myself, to men Useless.
>
> —Wordsworth, *The Prelude*

As universities rid themselves of the arts, humanities, and social sciences, they become glorified vocational schools for those seeking jobs in tech or business. One might object that there is no human interest in the skills developed in such schools, but at least the people are employed, we're told, and they're getting the "good jobs."

But even that logic is in doubt when so many students find that entry-level employment has been monopolized by AI, and, amid the West's never ending Industrial Revolution, by automation. This reality is leaving tens of thousands of people, heads full of expensive skills that nobody wants or needs, living in their childhood bedrooms or their parents' basement, gloomily doomscrolling through the day, wondering how in the world their student loans will ever be repaid, and feeling just generally unneeded and unwanted.

Not surprisingly, the consequences for mental health have been bad. According to a 2023 Gallup poll, 47 percent of Gen Z adults are anxious or depressed "often or always" because of social media, financial stress, and isolation.

But the numbers are, indeed, brow-raising: in late 2025, the unemployment rate among college graduates stood at nearly 6 percent, while the general unemployment rate was just over 4 percent. So, why go to college at all? Sure, apprentice to one of the trades. Go for construction, as if there were no downside to manual labor. It's like the scene at the end of *Office Space* in which Peter makes the discovery that the emptiness of office work has led him to a life with shovel in hand.

> Peter: "This isn't so bad, huh? Makin' bucks. Workin' outside. Gettin' exercise."
>
> Lawrence: "Fuckin' A."

Techno-capitalism's circle in hell is the hole (or parental basement) of the Empty Self. Imagine Dante walking in this hell, wondering about the devilish devices that the damned are staring into, fingers flying, and Virgil commenting, "They're looking for themselves."

Dante asks, "What are they seeing, master?"

Virgil replies, "Ghosts."

"And what sin did they commit for this punishment?"

"Their sin was their lifelessness."

Virgil has Bob Dylan's "Desolation Row" on heavy rotation.

Gen-Z youth imagine that their future is dependent on studying subjects for which they have no living interest. They have only the failing assumption that writing code, analyzing data, programming, or engineering software will eventually lead to prosperous material lives, or just survival, no matter how dull the reality is.

This is made even more hellish by the fact that the people in it are alone. My generation had to disengage from television, but a life lived online is another level of insidious alienation and, worse yet, it is all on the inside, eroding inner life, leaving nothing for the soul, nothing for soul-work, everything for addictive pleasure and profit. As David Foster Wallace commented in a 1996 interview with David Lipsky for *Rolling Stone*, sounding out a now familiar doom:

> At a certain point we're gonna have to build up some machinery, inside our guts, to help us deal with this. The technology is just gonna get better and better and better and better. And it's gonna get easier and easier and more and more convenient, and more and more pleasurable, to be alone with images on a screen, given to us by people who do not love us but want our money . . . If we don't do that, then (a) as individuals, we're gonna die, and (b) the culture's gonna grind to a halt.

But Wallace didn't mean to blame the young. The difference between Gen Z and earlier generations is that our young have to suffer the effects of techno-alienation much more intensely because the technology has indeed gotten "better and better and better." And they will be caught within it for a much longer time, and without the helpful memory of any sort of "time before tech." Perhaps this is why Gen Z is currently experiencing a paradoxical nostalgia for the analogue world of the 1990s.

Well, then, what are we to do? How about, "Workers of the world, relax! Make yourselves useless, you have nothing to lose but your virtual chains!"

In *On Tyranny*, Timothy Snyder asks us to say no to rising fascism by preserving liberal democratic institutions. But he never imagines that there might be reasons to say no to those institutions, to our "managers of despair," as well. He offers little understanding of the importance of a resistant culture, innately anarchic, opposing all that is anti-human. Resistant cultures seek to provide a place where we can become who we really are, a place where we are not mere functions of the world we happened to be born into, not diminished creatures whose being has been reduced to a marketable "skill set."

Resistant cultures work through honesty, intelligence, and beauty. They ask of us what Buddha asked of his followers: listen, consider, and cultivate. Listen to what we have discovered; consider what you have heard; and if you like what you have heard and considered, if it speaks to you, then join with others in the *sangha*, the Buddhist community, where you can cultivate a path that others in their turn may follow. This is the ideal way to join any human group: not by thoughtlessly inhabiting its damaged forms and conditions, but by freely engaging, considering, choosing, and, with this freedom in place, making something beautiful.

As Thich Nhat Hanh taught, "The next Buddha will be a Sangha."

## TAKE BACK YOUR EMPTINESS: 7 THESES ON RESISTANCE

Value haunts my being.

—**Jean-Paul Sartre**

1. Our politics are a binary melodrama: humanist against evangelical, Democrat against Republican, socialist against fascist, Woke against racist, Kimmel against Trump, comedians against reality-show celebrities. By dominating the stage, these dramas exclude other ways of understanding who we are and what we want, in other words, what we lack.

2. These melodramatic struggles distract us from the real question—what values shall we live by? Our

true values are not to be found in what we think, or in what we say we believe, but in how we live.

3. This contradicts the idea, common among us, that we are a free country rich in belief. "I believe X," we are told, with the expectation that others will respect that belief, even if it makes no sense. It is as if belief has been reserved only for the unbelievable.

4. The value we live through in the present moment is no different from the foundational value of ancient Greece and Rome: the "right of conquest." This may sound hyperbolic, but the people of Gaza, Venezuela, and even Greenland understand it well. This value instructs friend and foe alike, "You can do whatever you want on the condition that you make your desires fit my ends . . . or else." As Trump aide Stephen Miller acknowledged in a CNN interview in January of 2026, "We live in a world . . . that is governed by strength, that is governed by force, that is governed by power." Vae victis, woe to the victims.

5. The worst psychopathology of everyday life is to be treated unjustly and not to know it. This injustice inevitably concerns money, its inequities, and its specious allure. Buddhist philosopher David Loy writes, "Money is the flight from emptiness that

makes life empty." This is the truth, but it is also something that we don't know.

6. Rather than seeing emptiness as a mark of failure, can we see it as something to reclaim? Emptiness is a fundamental human joy if we feel free to respond to it. Freedom to play, to create, to live in our own strength. As Tibetan Buddhist Tarthang Tulku thought, "Life is the play of energy in the void." Children are primed for life through play, but their play only prepares them for a world that doesn't exist.

7. Jesus was a heretic because he hated hypocrites, those whose "throats were open graves." In Nietzsche's estimation, this made him "the noblest of men." Jesus made himself useless to the ways of the Temple and useless to the ways of Empire. He encouraged us to take back our emptiness from the ethical absolutes of the Mosaic Law and from the false gods of Rome. He began the very human remaking of his Father's earthly kingdom without any ethical guidance beyond the primordial aspirations of love. As Saint Augustine taught, simply, "Love and do what you will."

Make yourself useless! Take back your emptiness! Make something beautiful!

## FORGET THE BEATLES

> God is afoot
> Magic is alive
> Alive is afoot
> Magic never died.
> —**Buffy Sainte-Marie, "God is Alive, Magic is Afoot"**

I have written this manifesto in what Vladimir Nabokov called "a state of aesthetic bliss," which he defined as:

> a sense of being somehow, somewhere, connected with other states of being where art (curiosity, tenderness, kindness, ecstasy) is the norm.

That's the hill I intend to die on, for all the good intending will do me. Because that hill may already be gone. I have reclined in its grasses for so long—gazing down on moving water, assuming that all I had to do was turn and I'd be looking up toward the crest—that I may have missed the moment when the earthmovers came in, noisy though they are, and the mountaintop removal began. And then a guy in an orange vest and a hard hat comes up and explains to me that, "Son, you're living in the world of yesterday."

Stefan Zweig's complaint in *The World of Yesterday* was exactly this: A form of moral beauty had disappeared beneath him and he was left suspended in air. As Goth Rock legend Robert Smith of The Cure sings in "Endsong," the last song on their album *Songs of a Lost World* (2024): it's gone, gone, "Nothing left of all I loved."

And yet, I hope that this book in its playfulness, its non-linear anarchy, expresses not a longing for the work of the past but energy for the future. Not illustrations for an ideology, but the pure energy of world-making. In a sense, we need to "Forget the Beatles" and the countercultures they inspired. Presently, that culture lives only a gray half-life through Spotify playlists, Hollywood biopics about Dylan and the Doors (et tu, Led Zep?), and the blasphemous productions of corporate giants like Universal Music Group, selling us our own past. That music has been, in tech parlance, the victim of "enshittification," the apotheosis of which will be that quickly approaching time when music's "zone" is flooded with AI slop. As one AI music generator named "imoliver" commented, "I have no musical talent at all. I can't sing, I can't play instruments, and I have no musical background." All this under the cover of "democratizing song-making," never mind that the mark of the best music has heretofore been its soulful heresies. What was once alive and full of the warmth of sharing is now only about creating a brand and making a buck in a world where anyone, anywhere, could make the next big hit.

You've heard of the Land of Cockaigne, that fanciful place where abundance reigns. Well, welcome to the Land of Cliché, where AI rummages through all that has been said and sung and then throws it against the wall to see what sticks.

Someone should be ashamed, but we're all too excited about this brave new world to know it.

The arts need to de-shittify and return to peasant energies, ready to be changed, changed utterly, into something a new generation can live in and live through. In the Imagination, a new comedy will rise, because its loving playfulness, its caring embrace of others, is always with us, regardless of every inhuman distortion of the world as it stands. Hegel called this comedy the "World in Love." Ultimately, that is what Nietzsche's "transvaluation of all values" seeks, too: love not as an ethical command but as an artful metaphysic.

> Suddenly it is at an end. THE WORLD IS NEW!"
>
> —**William Carlos Williams,** ***Spring and All***

## ABOUT THE AUTHOR

CURTIS WHITE is a novelist and social critic whose works include *Transcendent*, *Living in a World That Can't Be Fixed*, *The Science Delusion*, and *Memories of My Father Watching TV*. His essays have appeared in *Harper's*, *Lapham's Quarterly*, *Salon*, and *Tricycle*. He is the founder with Ronald Sukenick of FC2, a publisher of innovative fiction run collectively by its authors. He lives in Port Townsend, WA.

## ACKNOWLEDGEMENTS

"Psychic Treason" first appeared in *CounterPunch*.

"The Philanthropic Industrial Complex" first appeared in *Jacobin* and *Lapham's Quarterly*.

"Technically, It's Enshittification" first appeared in *Tricycle*.

"The End of the Liberal Arts Dream" first appeared in *Salon*.

"The Late Word" first appeared in *Lapham's Quarterly*.